D1422872

SCOTT
AND THE
LURE OF THE ROAD

SCOTT
AND THE
LURE OF THE ROAD

BY

THE REV. P. LAURENCE K. MUDIE

LONDON
JAMES CLARKE & COMPANY, LIMITED
9 ESSEX STREET, STRAND, W.C. 2
1932

Printed in Great Britain

TO THE UNIVERSITY AND HIGH SCHOOL
OF THE SCOTTISH CAPITAL

"Ay, yonder is the heart of Scotland"
The Abbot

PREFACE

EACH of the Novels may be studied with a friendly Map in front of us. It has been the literary recreation of the writer for many years, to go over the actual ground of the best known of the Wizard's Tales, and to gather from the surroundings the real background of each. The serious attempt is made in this book, to link the environment to the romantic setting of Scott's writings. There are some authors who merely imagine scenes. Scott's skill is seen at its best as he mirrors them. Places and people stand out in true perspective. England and Scotland are reproduced in his Novels, in the wealth of hamlet and of moorland, of city and of vale.

The advantages of this method of studying his works are evident. It gives the reader a much more detailed interest in his own country. He finds himself in most varied parts of Britain with a peculiar sense of being at home, because Scott has already been before him in his quest. The author of *Waverley* has consecrated this unfamiliar ground to a new purpose. Figures of the past look out on the visitor from the ruins of old castles and monasteries. They pass down the streets of ancient towns. They wage their warfare on forgotten battle-fields. They carry to this somewhat prosaic age something of the glamour of a too easily receding past.

Preface

Such questions as these are naturally related to Craftsmanship. We cannot consider them without making an effort to analyse the art which they both reveal and conceal. This volume, without rehearsing the critical estimates of the last hundred years, at least suggests how that criticism may be summarised. In the last analysis, Craftsmanship is related to Personality and Character. We shall invite the reader to consider the Creed of Sir Walter Scott, and to find his religious outlook persuasively and almost unconsciously weaving itself into his classic narratives, and expressing itself in the *dramatis personæ*. Many other writers have made an attempt to estimate the spirit and attitude of Scott. It is not so usual to find efforts made to discover this high ethical standard, moulding the habit and affecting the speech of laird and cottar, soldier and priest. We cannot make this exploration through the Waverley Novels without assessing the Writer's place in the philosophy of the period, and enthroning him in that literary eminence to which his unrivalled worth entitles him for ever to linger.

The Author wishes cordially to thank Professor Baxter of St. Andrews, and Dr. Gavin, Lecturer in History in the University of Aberdeen. These scholars have been most helpful in their suggestions, as the book passed through the press.

CONTENTS

PART I

PART II

Contents

PART I

CHAPTER I

HIS CRAFTSMANSHIP

MANY minds are awake to the splendour of Scott's
lore. For long the world of thinking men has
been spellbound by his tales. There is often
need in the realm of letters of a recapture of its
coveted fields of fancy. The Centenary is an
intellectual impulse to reading folk to realise more
fully the treasure that is in their midst.

The critic is never far away. The modernist
particularly in exalting the novel of to-day is
emphatic as to the defects of the Georgian period.
He accuses it of lacking in technique. He joins
issue with the want of finished phrasing. He tilts
his weapon at the uncareful writer of circuitous
prose. There may be occasionally room for these
innuendoes. Nevertheless there is a development
of the novel. There is a historic sense in which all
works that are not contemporary should be assessed.
Saintsbury long ago remarked sanely that he levelled
no protest at criticism either of Shakespeare or of
Scott. Nothing criminal lay to his mind in adverse
comment. The crime was rather, he felt, in the
method of approach, in the way the criticism was
done.

We can all recall at the University certain of our

teachers who dissected a work of art with the broad
blade of invective—and it perhaps marred for long
the works from which we fain had profited. There
were other preceptors who without ignoring the
flaws taught us to love the beauty. To this hour
we are more indebted to them than we ever could
be to the ruthless assailant. Constructive appreciation is more difficult, and more pleasing than
incisive comment.

All the original writers whose charm delights,
and whose wisdom profits, have been men who
built upon the stable foundations of the past.
They were awake to the false structure, and the
inapt adornment of architecture. They built better
than they knew, when they acknowledged the
worth of those who had planned in previous decades.
The masonry to which they applied their skill is
a product of yesterday. Scott was foremost in the
admission of this. He studied Fielding and
Smollett, Sterne, Goldsmith and Johnson.

He lingers over the pages of Richardson, Mrs.
Radcliffe and Maria Edgeworth. Austin Dobson
in his preface to Scott's *Biographies of the Novelists*
has a happy note. "There was nothing about Scott
of the critical seed-splitters. No juster nor more
open-minded censor—none kinder, more capable
nor more considerate ever sat in the seat of
Aristarchus."

Lockhart too has borne the same witness. He
has a graceful reference to that "perpetual stream
of deep and gentle wisdom in commenting on the
tempers and fortunes of his best predecessors
in novel literature." He admits how profoundly
" Scott had investigated the principles and practice

of those masters before he struck out a new path for himself." The logic of all this is apparent. If he is the object in these days of somewhat slighting disdain by a few of our rising authors, are they just ? In the development of their own technique, in the untold store of Romance with which he has enriched them, does it become them to be less fair to their precursors than he was to the encompassing host with which he was surrounded ?

Down to the actual month when we write of him, his words are quoted. In the very last work of Dean Inge, theologian and mystic, appear words from *Rob Roy*. Wherever we have a great mind to portray, there is ever, as in all art, something that is indefinable. Personality is an elusive item. We may explain the origin of plots. We may suggest the assumed originals of leading figures. We may stage the drama. We may create the background. When we have done all, we have to deal with the reaction on the artist's spirit. Why does his model impress him as it does ? What by-play of fancy clothes his heroes in such guise that they become to us like our own personal friends ? Take up four of the best novels in succession. Create before your mind's eye the setting. Make each dialogue and stirring act live before you. The *dramatis personæ* cease to be mere figures in a play. They take on flesh and blood. When we lay down each volume, there linger in our gallery of recollection pictures of enduring loveliness. The men and women who have conversed in our presence by the fireside, as we read, are possibly more known to us and beloved even than our next-door neighbour. To say when our task is complete how they have been painted on that magnificent canvas, is to attempt to explain mystery. There are certain elemental things in all drama—joy, birth, sorrow, misunderstanding, the shadow unfathomed, the light immortal. These may be presented to us. The better they are focussed the less the artist and the spectator are able to tell how the oracle is worked.

In writing this, we do not for a moment ignore the duty that is placed before us. We welcome it. For the discovery of our quest is bound to affect our own toil. No one can even imperfectly attempt to assess the craftsmanship without insensibly becoming more effective in his own daily task. In teaching, in speaking, in reading, in preaching, in a score of lawful employments, he takes on something of the majesty of the company that he keeps.

Our plea is, that in the study of the work of Scott, we have not made sufficient of the local colouring of the surroundings that he describes. We know how when he was questioned on the locale of some of his tales he only made some enigmatic reply or smiled. We may be often far astray in fixing too rigidly the favoured spot where his imagination first began to weave its wondrous garment. Yet we feel that he knew these Isles of ours well. Britain in its length and breadth was familiar to him. No one who is versed in his novels but has dwelt, if not in person at least in mental contact, amid the countryside or by the archives where his literary ardour first had its birth.

A literary friend who knew the Borders wrote to him from Grasmere in October, 1803—" We passed Branxholme, your Branxholme we supposed, about four miles on this side of Hawick. It looks better in your poem than in its present realities." In other words he was not an abstract thinker. He knew of such studies as philosophy, and he is often profound in his allusions to the deepest things in human life and destiny. His was the soul that rather concealed his deeper emotions. He did not live merely in a world of ideas, but of fact. He knew men. He had a marvellous insight into human nature. How firmly had his heroes and heroines their feet planted on Mother Earth.

CHAPTER II

OLD MORTALITY AND LANARKSHIRE

It is perhaps the love of fair play to an unpopular cause that has made *Old Mortality* misunderstood. Ever since the protests of Dr. McCrie, Scott has been charged with treating the Blue Banner with disdain. Yet there are sentences in the tale that are as high in praise of the Covenanter at his best, as the keenest partisan might have employed. Scott is not so much opposed to the movement as to its excess. He loved not too well the man who was righteous overmuch. If he ridicules Mause Headrigg, it is more for her insincerity than for her devotion to a cause. He distinguished the movement from some of its faltering and hypocritical adherents. Let the tourist dismount from his cycle on his way from Glencaple to Annan at the Tomb of Old Mortality. There will rush to memory Scott's admiring affection for this lover of the Whig Crusade. Where he saw genuine adherence, no one was more lavish in his praise. Where he saw a craven spirit or a boasting of superior goodness, then quite justly the figures came under the condemning rod. Here again, we have to live by the scenes to appreciate the worth of the Romance, to walk by Clydeside, to cross the Brig, to loiter by the ruined walls of Craignethan, to walk through Darvel and peep at our own famous Loudon hill. We may watch the waves of the

Old Mortality and Lanarkshire

Moray Firth from Banff Castle, where Archbishop Sharpe was born. Even "a beauteous soil like Banff," says Dr. Crammond, "may produce a noisome weed." Then we speed to Magus Muir and trace the defaced Latin on the inscription where the Prelate was unjustly murdered.

It is then that Lanarkshire, as pictured by the novelist, opens its treasure house to us. It is then that we are prepared to see the real sequence of the tale, and to follow the tortuous steps of Balfour of Burleigh and of Morton. Is this recorder a prejudiced Royalist after all ? How does he portray dedicated scenes that are the prelude to Drumclog ? Who that really scorned the Covenanter could have depicted their open-air Temple ? They have the rocks for their altar. The sky was their vaulted sanctuary. Their swords were instruments for sacrifice. Is there not the magic of the visionary in his apt rehearsal of a now ancient battle, when Heaven fought for us as the stars in their courses against Sisera ? When *Old Mortality* was written, a schoolboy wrote to him and said, "Oh, Sir Walter, how could you take the lady from the gallant Cavalier and give her to the prick-eared Covenanter ? " Yet if Sir Walter had really detested the Whig as his critics attempt to make out, his romance had been otherwise ordered.

Remember Bessie Maclure. Does not every reader love the old, blind woman in the hillside cottage ? Is it not Scott's discerning eye for the nobler soul in the Covenanter that makes us love her too ? Her eyes are dimmed of mortal sight, but she sees into the eternal. Her movements are timid and her body is pained, but she has a supporting arm for Lord Evandale in his wounds—though her own sons had met death from her enemies. Someone has truly said " that the charm of Bessie Maclure is as deathless as the men and women of Shakespeare." May we not pardon one who thus pictures the best on the Presbyterian side, even if he does not ignore the valour of Claverhouse ? On climbing the stair to the old study at Tweedside, the portrait rivets the admiration of the keenest hater of Prelacy. What a face of radiant worth ! What loyalty to a cause that he dreamt at least to be just ! In his portraiture of Bonnie Dundee, history at least is on the side of Scott when he sketches him as a man of the rarest courage—even if he were misled. A recently published record in which his last words at Killiecrankie are rehearsed is worth quoting—" How goes the day ? " " Well for the King," is the answer, " but I am sorry for your Lordship." " 'Tis the less matter," whispers Graham, " 'Tis the less matter for me, seeing the day goes well for my master."

If the painting of that figure appear not without prejudice, if his be an undeserved halo, we may recall this feature in the craftsmanship of Scott. He had a judicial mind, as well as the seeing heart. He did not allow even the play of emotion to render unbalanced his estimate of the real worth even of an unbridled crusade.

As a craftsman, one of his best instruments is his language. A correspondent of Sir Walter's, a shepherd of Ettrick Forest, who knew Scotch well and was himself a son of the soil, wrote him under date, June, 1820—" I cannot help telling you that I am astonished, perfectly astonished how ye have acquired the Scottish dialect and phraseology so exactly. Certainly neither your education or studies could discover aught of that antiquated language. Yet when ye choose to adopt it, ye have it as truly as if ye knew no other, but had lived in the nook of the Forest all your life." In novels such as *Old Mortality*, the reader feels how much this contact with Scottish dialect, feeling and manners, has added to the reality of the scenes. The craftsmanship has in it the atmosphere not of the detached on-looker, but of the actual pilgrim to Bothwell Brig and the Nethan. Tillietudlem was a fortified manor house of the Evandale branch of the Hamilton family. On his visit there in 1799 Scott was charmed with the surroundings. Lord Douglas, learning this, suggested to him that if he cared, the Castle farmhouse should be his for life. It is this rich knowledge of surroundings—this detailed portraiture—that gives the touch of reality to his background. The haunting love of the past yields the clue to the verse in praise of the original of *Old Mortality*. The lines are equally apropos of the creator of the tale :

> " Why seeks he with unwearied toil,
>   Through death's dim walks to urge his way ?
> Reclaim his long asserted spoil,
>   And lead oblivion into day ? "

Yet his is no morbid love of the tomb. His face is always to the dawn, to the pressing life of the morrow. Not death, but the heritage that it yields, this is the key to his devotion to history. We remember how he makes his soldier hero say, "It is not the expiring pang that is worth thinking of.

Scott and the Lure of the Road

It is the memory which the soldier leaves behind him. It is like the long train of light that follows the sinking sun. It is this which is worth caring for, which distinguishes the death of the brave and the noble."

If this Essay is burdened by any message to the reader of Scott, it is that his art is largely dependent on his knowledge of surroundings. These provide the scenic effects for his genius. It is true, of course, that these things do not explain the art. Yet it is when the local colouring in the tales is seen by the traveller that something of the marvel of his skill is revealed.

The nearer that we come to the scenes that he describes on coast-line and by mountain-side, the more nigh do we come to Scott himself. He is part of them. He is weaved into the texture of our love and loyalty to the homeland. There is no chord so deep in the human spirit as the impulse that binds us to our native shores. It is the echo of all that is best in man until he dies. A poet has mystically spoken of the dwelling of our early childhood thus— "home which our feet may leave, but not our hearts." We are never far from these idyllic days if we are in Scott's company.

It is worth while to linger by the scenes of *Old Mortality*, for if we accustom ourselves to that habit of mind which senses the literary atmosphere in this instance, then it prepares us to do so in all the other novels. We find our locus here by Clydeside, in Lanarkshire. We passed a little inn a few miles from Hamilton. It has the popinjay as its ensign. It claims to be in the centre of that rich countryside where the famous wappinschaw was held. The deep flowing river, the broad fields, the proximity to Craignethan and to Milton-Lockhart which Scott knew so well, entitle us to think of it as a likely scene for these contests. We can well imagine Edith Bellenden and Henry Morton as they exchanged glances on the day of Morton's triumph. We can picture Lord Balfour of Burleigh in his association with the district and his ride to Milnwood.

It is quite the quiet pastoral spot that lends itself to the artist who images a retreat for the murderer of Sharpe. What consternation in these restful surroundings when it is known that the head of the retreating Burleigh is worth its weight in gold to his accusers! No finer setting than Tillietudlem could be found for the background of *Old Mortality*. We readily link Claverhouse and his soldiers with its old family traditions. Its high and precipitous condition, its piles of masonry, its stable defences, its moat and drawbridge, make it till this day the marvel of all the admiring visitors who haunt it. We still seem to hear amid its ruined apartments the strident tones of Jenny Dennison in her alarm at Cuddie Headrigg's approach. So real does it all seem to those who love Craignethan that the supposed window is still pointed out where that enterprising Scottish lass performed the warlike baptism of broth upon the too ardent assailant! This at least is a witness that, however unfounded in history certain living deeds of fiction are, the hand of Scott is so skilled that people actually associate outward surroundings even with the fancies that he has weaved.

If we were indulging in any psychological

analysis, we would be tempted to enquire if the work of the true dramatist does not really alter for us the whole question of reality. History is surely not the one inevitable canon of truth. Truth is discovered not merely in its adherence to actual facts, but also in fidelity to vital experience, and in its interpretation of human nature. Although Cuddie Headrigg may never have climbed that giddy ascent to the Castle, and although Jenny never boldly defended its walls, the picture that Scott has drawn is a reflection of life. Is not this an artist's work to accomplish ? Does it not prove that places in all their picturesque surroundings were more to him than he was sometimes aware of ? Tillietudlem had an extraordinary fascination for him. Even in Italy, he recalled its loveliness. Readers of Lockhart will recall how Lanarkshire and its beauty was the subject of his talk in Naples. We can imagine that playful smile making sunlight on his face as he dwelt again on the siege. Was it not the quaint Cuddie of his earlier dreams who had confessed to " creeping in at the window whiles to get some daffin' at e'en after the pleugh was loosed " ? Great enterprises give the Wizard his fine opportunity of glowing description. Every reader will admit that sometimes the less pretentious scenes that give us glimpses of simple, homelier life reveal as nobly his sympathy and skill.

Those who write on Tillietudlem speak of the strength of its site. It is admitted that before the days of artillery it was impregnable. There is an old tradition of a subterranean vault which reached the level of the Nethan. It is conjectured that by this means the rivulet supplied the garrison with water under a siege. There is a personal touch in the writer's description that is full of interest. Scott wrote of course as a Royalist, but he was fully acquainted with the traditions of the Whig. Andrew Lang brought to light a letter which rehearsed some of the novelist's memories of talks with his kinsmen about tales of these days of rebellion handed down to him. His father's grandmother used to attend the hill preaching of the Covenanters. She remembered the ladies sitting in their side-saddles which were taken off their horses and placed for convenience on the grass. She recollected the zealous clergyman finding a pulpit in the rugged rocks, and thundering forth his somewhat severe doctrine with more vehemence than a little girl could well appreciate. Scott had met Paterson, the original of *Old Mortality*, at Dunnottar. It is not to be wondered at if readers simply went into raptures when such a tale as this came from the press. Murray, the printer, once asked Lord Holland his opinion of this story and he replied that all the last night none of them had gone to bed. It would be a great thing for the somewhat material age in which we live, if that intense love for romanticism could revive. If we learn to live in a world different from our own, if we bridge the great gulfs which time and space make as mental barriers for us, we are doing much for our inner perception. There can be no doubt that the actual touring of the counties that are wedded to the novels is one of the most helpful means to this renaissance. It is an important means by which the study of English literature will be vitalised. When we are in the company of Scott we are with a man whose mind is stored with the lore of the ages, with the quaint customs and sayings of a treasured past. He brings us as naturally as does a child to laughter and to tears, to reverie and to pain. For it is life in its elemental guises that he unveils to us. If we would know the Infinite, then we must approach Him by the common path of the creatures whom He has made.

Characters analysed with minute skill are the more impressive because of the background. In the survey of Balfour of Burleigh, it is admitted by those who have sifted the data that it is no lack of generosity that prompts Scott to depict him as he does. Edith Bellenden is stately but somewhat detached. For this novelist is often more effective in the heroines that he paints from ordinary life. If they are nearer the soil, and the more menial task, they show better their kinship with humanity. None can but admire the chivalry and large-heartedness of Lord Evandale towards Morton. It may be argued that in his self-sacrificing courtesy he is also attempting to pay his rival the debt that he owes him for his life. Yet Evandale is himself the initiator of these kindly acts. Morton is the first to admit that the walls of Tillietudlem are hallowed for him by the intercessions of the Royalist in that critical hour when no other voice but Evandale's could have saved the man who had sheltered Burleigh.

Bothwell Brig, Drumclog, and that rich tract of country in the West, are redolent to us of a brave struggle, and of the story on both sides of many a gallant act of heroism. When we read the discourses of Kettledrummle they may seem far apart from the spirit of Lambeth, revealed in this day of grace. Yet may it not be that these stern conflicts in debate which characterised that time are the needful discipline by which we have been brought to the sense of the worth of unity? Morton is the type of the more catholic-minded man who pierced beneath the details in the bitter controversy, to extract the perennial truth. Balfour professed to be the champion of reformation, and the gathering of the dispersed saints. Morton had the spirit of reasonable compromise by which alone any mediating process can come about. These are noble words in which he speaks of his attitude to Scripture : " I look into them with humble hope of extracting a rule of conduct, and a law of salvation. I expect to find this by an examination of their general tenour, and of the spirit which they universally breathe, and not by wrestling particular passages from their context, or by the application of scriptural phrases to circumstances and events with which they have often very slender relation." If we visit the County of Lanark, it will be a means of deepening within us our sense of stewardship which the past has yielded us. It is a happy reflection that when, in this generation, a Scottish Churchman visits the Archbishop's Palace, he slumbers quietly at nightfall, undisturbed, in the room which bears the name of Archbishop Laud !

We may search in vain for Black Linn on the map. Skene admits that it is the creation of Scott's marvellous fancy. To read of Burleigh's sojourn there is to see the depths of depression which a dominant mind may reach, if it lose the gift of charity. Edmund Spenser has similarly pictured a despairing soul :

> " The darksome cave they enter, where they found,
> The accursed man low sitting on the ground,
> Musing full sadly in his sullen mind."

The dialogue which has its setting on the flat rock a hundred feet above the yawning chasm there is illustrative of the tension with which minds in these days were disturbed by grave religious problems. The strong red light glancing on the waves of the falling water, the awesome figure of the dejected leader are a strange contrast to the gentle voice of the little child who guided Morton to this rendezvous, and who told him " to tak' tent to his feet." Scott is sometimes at his best when he is an unconscious artist. Is it a subtlety of appreciative criticism to suggest that the novelist in face of insoluble problems often felt himself like a little child ? Bagehot in a most illuminating Essay stresses the common-sense view of Life and Religion which Scott takes. He wisely shows that if there are those of us who have to face questions in the intellectual world that seem to have no answer, it is a mental rest to dwell by his side. There is more inwardness in that figure of the little child at Black Linn than is always recognised. Geographically we may not be able to trace the locus on the map. Spiritually, the picture has a meaning for all time.

CHAPTER III

THIS novel has its locus in Derbyshire and in the
Isle of Man, in Liverpool and in London. It is in
the Peak District of England that the devotee will
most readily find his introduction to the environs
of the book. There he comes to wide moorland,
to shining river, to quaint, ancient villages. He
will find it an advantage to be in touch with the
ancient churches. They are often contemporary
with the period that he is studying. They stand
at the centre of the people's life. In some of their
buildings are treasured records of old families.
When he approaches Castleton, which is the small
hamlet which lies under the shadow of the home
of Peveril, he will find that this household has
sacred memorials preserved within the shrine.
It was here that Sir Geoffrey worshipped. As
he comes into the antique rooms, the literary
explorer will feel at once a sense of kinship with the
manners and the speech of the days of King Charles.
In the book we find the side of the Throne matched
against that of the Roundheads. There are on its
pages magnetic descriptions of that unforgettable
conflict in English history. If he wander in some
leisured moment by Dovedale, he will surprise
himself with the wondrous contrast to the scenes
of warfare of which the story is so full. In that
restful valley he is in the companionship of Izaak

Scott and the Lure of the Road

Walton in his *Compleat Angler*. Indeed it will come with a measure of restfulness to him to dip into that old classic that he may the better brace his spirit for following Scott to the sound of the trumpet, and the clash of the sword. *Peveril of the Peak* is a chronicle of brave warriors ; and a reader gains a truer perspective of life if he turn sometimes from war to the still waters which Walton loved.

Aid is given to the lover of research in a volume on Castleton. It traces the names and the records from 1645 to 1837. It is written by W. H. Shawcross, Vicar of Bretforton. The reader may have often wondered why that picturesque district of the Peak has any place for miners. When he has read Scott's novel, he may have felt that it is a kind of intrusion to introduce them in the narrative. His doubts will be dispelled if he visit the county. The lead-mines are all mentioned in the registers of the old Norman church. There are still immense mines with miles of caverns. Cotton, the poet, referred to them in 1682 :

> " Now to the cave we come, wherein is found
> A new strange thing, a village underground."

Queen Victoria was one of the visitors ; so was Byron, and a host of other celebrities. The old castle in which Sir Geoffrey lived is now in ruins. It has a commanding position on a summit, a fitting place for an eagle to build her nest. It overlooks the broad domains of a lovely country-side. To visit it is to people it with the stalwart figures that Scott's imagination has clothed in such living guise. The sway of this old soldier was wide and majestic ; and he wielded his sceptre far beyond the confines of the county. A member of the opposite political party stayed not many miles away. Peveril's Castle is called Martindale in the book, and the rival seat is Moultrassie. It was held by a certain Bridgenorth, who had made Peveril his debtor by loans of money in time of need. There was born at Moultrassie a little girl, but the joy of that hour was shadowed by the loss of his wife. As we pass his old home to-day, we reflect how great a comfort his daughter Alice might have been to him. In bitterness of soul and in revolt against Providence, he refused to let the cheer of her presence enter his life. Lady Peveril forgot old scores and enmities. She received Alice into her home of Martindale Castle. As we wander through the ruins on a summer day, we seem to see the light on the faces of Julian her son and Alice as they play together. What if their friendship may have wider bearings on the fortunes of the households than they know? Day by day, they are together in that once luxuriant dwelling. In the free frolic of the hillsides and of the nursery, they become sharers of each other's fate. Martindale has about it a stately kind of splendour. It carries with it all the halo of the stern times in which it was so prominent a centre. Above the warring notes of disputants and the clash of arms, we seem to turn instinctively to those intervals of peace when hope and love and laughter ring through the halls, and for the moment battle is forgotten.

Yet that happiness is not long in being disturbed. As the children play, a majestic figure enters through a concealed doorway. This is the Countess of Derby, who had sailed in a moment of peril from her stronghold in the Isle of Man. What has happened to demand her presence here?

William Christian is a brother-in-law of Bridgenorth. He has proved disloyal to the Countess in the Isle of Man, where she is the acknowledged queen. As a penalty for his insubordination, he is condemned to death. We stood by the somewhat weird spot on the famous Isle where Christian was made a victim of the rude justice of these times. Certainly the plea of this Volume is readily furthered in relation to the actual scenes where acts in that stirring era took place. We here touch history. We are on ground where the name of Christian is reverently remembered. Curiously enough, Scott had never visited the Isle. He had imbued much of the worth of the place, its folk-lore, its native customs, as well as the splendour of the scenery from Mr. Train. He had also learned of it from Thomas, his brother. Christian was in a delicate position. He had to act as the representative of a population as well as on his own initiative. No unbiassed student can acquit the Countess of somewhat dire measures in her treatment of her Dempster.

She has come for refuge to Martindale, where she can count on the friendly shelter of Sir Geoffrey. When the children's alarm is somewhat allayed, her explanations are made. Bridgenorth, who naturally resents her action towards his relative, wishes her to be seized, and brought before the judges. Sir Geoffrey intervenes, and leads her away to a place of safety. It is also arranged that Julian goes over at a later stage to the Isle to be a companion of her son. It is an almost necessary tour, if we would catch the spirit of the book, to visit that Isle. We may revel in the magnificent coast-line, its old castles and abbeys. We stand on one favoured spot in a cathedral aisle where the date shows a year at least contemporary with Canterbury. Man is intimately related with Derby both in history and in the tale. Even names of places, such as Castleton, occur in both. We gain a deeper sense of the loftiness of Peel, at the mouth of the Neb, its piles of masonry, its commanding site overlooking the wide ocean, the steps where Fenella made her fairy-like descents. As we cross over the intervening stream on a stormy day from the village adjoining, we gain a deeper sense of the unrivalled defences of such a stronghold in time of war. Julian became acquainted with the inner workings of its civil administration, with its subtle contacts with England and the Court of Charles. In daily companionship with the son of the Countess, he was versed in intrigue. Somehow, when we tread the Isle and enter into the mystic glamour that it casts upon the serious pilgrim, it is easier to look on the wide canvas of Scott's description in *Peveril of the Peak* with an appreciative eye. Yet it is not only the manœuvre of the courtier that interests us. Black Fort is the scene of Julian's romantic hours. When grown to be a sturdy youth, he discovers that Alice is resident here ; and many a lengthy converse is theirs. Will they be the sharers of each other's fortunes, or has fate ordained that their lives (once so happily merged in childhood's sunny hours) will be set far apart ? Bridgenorth has come to stay on the Isle; and he intervenes in a critical moment to give a ray of hope to them when Alice is inclined to feel that the civil strife has eclipsed all her hopes. Fenella's wiles are more rapidly pictured when we enter into her surroundings here. We can image to ourselves more readily the irritating treatment she inflicted on Julian, the trial to his patience when she persistently followed him. It is not till long after, when we know that her dumbness and deafness are only feigned, and that she is a daughter of Christian in disguise, that we see the source of her clever stratagems, and her uncanny knowledge of events. Avowedly in the service of the Countess, she is able to mould events by her compliance in plot, and in purpose alien to the rule and spirit of her mistress's regime. All this clever acting is partly the effect of the concealed position that she holds, and also of the peculiar geographical conditions which give her her place. That wondrous understanding which the author had of the background of his scenic effects, has a far more intimate play on the dramatic movement than critics are willing to admit. That power too that he possessed to delineate what he had never actually seen is noteworthy. We think of members of the pre-Raphaelite School spending years in the survey of detail which they embody in their minute workmanship. What shall we say of the artist in words who so portrays the Isle of Man as to impress the reader with the authentic environment? How shall we assess the skill with which he permits his figures to become part of that setting, as if they and the place of their dwelling are the spontaneous expression of a master-mind?

Julian is the emissary of the affairs of the Countess of Derby. He has to cross to England. It is not needful to follow him in his chequered experiences at the horse-market in Liverpool, at the Court of Charles, in companionship with Ganlesse as he rides across the country, or in his exploits in the London park. The local colouring of the book is most strikingly in evidence in the closing scenes at Martindale. In these troublous times there had been a serious rising of the Commonwealth followers against the house of Peveril. When Julian returned to Derbyshire, he was humbled and saddened to discover that his ancient home was in danger. He entered the inn. On its windows for generations there had been emblazoned the crest and armorial bearings of his family. When we came to Castleton to visit it, we were surprised to find the surroundings so similar to the description in the novel. We were told that if this be the inn of the tale, the surmise is a feasible conjecture when we consider its age. It has stood there for six hundred years. It still has the thick oak flooring, associated with the best of old English hostels, the perpendicular mantelpieces, and the general setting of such a place of call. When we climbed the stairway, it was almost as if the spirit of Julian still haunted the place. Again we seemed to listen to the ribald laughter of the soldiers, as they defied the authority of the royalist chief, and ignored the standing of his son.

Even more impressive is the reference that Scott makes to the light in the Castle. Never save on the internment of the owner had it been known to be extinguished. Julian's heart failed as he realised that no longer could he look upon its far-extended beams. It stood for three things—the sway of suzerainty over the county and far beyond it, the welcome to the benighted pilgrim, the symbol of Lady Peveril's love to her lord to cheer him on his homeward way. The tragical happenings of the hours of struggle in the darkened Castle, the riot of the revolters are acts in this Shakespearean-like drama that hold the attention of readers spellbound. Julian's fears, however, concerning the quenched light are unfounded. Happily, his father, though wounded and beset, still survives. The son has come in the moment when the peril is greatest, and deliverance is part of the ministry of grace that his coming yields. There is another light in his heart. He has never lost his attachment for Alice. Bridgenorth, her father, is now more catholic in his outlook, and he is willing at last to give his full consent to the marriage. It is his assumed connivance in the Popish Plot of Titus Oates that is the charge against Sir Geoffrey which casts its shadow on these hours of joy. Charles II is the generous assessor of the rights of his loyal and heroic soldier. Peveril is rescued from his accusers, and condoned by his judges. Julian and Alice are now the favoured children of fortune. The light in Martindale Castle shines again with its radiant rays. No one who visits that rich countryside goes away unmoved by the lingering memories which crowd upon his mind. Each traveller who carries *Peveril of the Peak* with him on his journeys finds in the far stretching landscape beauteous prospects. They are already familiar to him in the pages of Scott.

CHAPTER IV

CASTLE DANGEROUS——IN DOUGLAS DALE

If we have seen the etching of Douglas Castle Tower by Macbeth Raeburn, we shall require no further lure to linger by its ruins. Certainly there is not much to be seen of the ancient edifice. Even it is only a remnant of more antique piles, long since demolished. The place itself is fragrant of some of the most stirring scenes in Scottish story. The moment we enter the village we feel that we are treading on historic ground. There is flashed upon our mind the heroic chapter that is linked with the name of Bruce and his followers. Above all, there stands out in recollection the bold, strong figure of Sir James Douglas, who was one of the chief heralds of his reign as well as one of his most gallant soldiers.

By permission of His Grace the Earl of Home, we saw one of the oldest paintings of the good Sir James, and the broadsword presented to him by the King. These are now safely guarded in the Castle. There were stirred in us the inspiring thoughts that make this period so memorable in history. The narrow streets of Douglas are eloquent of a period when people were bound to hold well together for security. Ideas of health and house-planning were then over-shadowed by the impelling need of defence. In the darkness of the spring evening we could feel the sense of the mystery of that shadowed past. We

35

could hear the echo of the hoofs of the warrior's horse, and the wild cry of St. George on the one hand and Douglas on the other. For, still in Scotland there was the contest for the Throne. No one knew when Edward might assert his sovereignty. If we were inclined to forget for a moment why the Castle is called "Dangerous," deep below the chapel the reminder of it comes. There is the old well which was kept well defended in case of siege or fire. The thick walls and splendid position of the Castle, its courageous sentinels and guardians, made assault a more than hazardous undertaking. It has the attractions also of a rich and most healthy district. It stands many hundred feet above sea-level. Quite apart from the strategic ground that it occupies, it has a fascination for the visitor. He may let his wondering eye wander over a wealth of pasture-land, shining water and mountain slope. He ceases to marvel that Sir James coveted the joy and the honour of holding this Castle. For the loyalty to his King, of which it was the witness, was also the outward symbol of personal magnificence and power. Yet it fell into the hands of the English. The plot of Sir Walter Scott's tale turns to a large extent upon the grim struggle to possess it, as also on the romantic tale of love that indirectly restored it to the Scottish knight. There were circumstances in the life and in the state of health of the novelist when he wrote this tale that account for certain defects in treatment. If the reader desire to gain some knowledge of these, and if he grow a little weary reading Lockhart, let him see Winifred Gunn's attractive play when it is staged in his own town. In her *Scott of Abbotsford*,

Castle Dangerous—In Douglas Dale

Miss Gunn covers the period in our author's life when "his moving hand" worked less deftly. The drama that she has skilfully sketched is historically well founded, and it is dramatically effective. It is rich in deep emotion, and her background is artistically conceived.

If we wish to enjoy *Castle Dangerous* more fully we should seek to visit that picturesque countryside, to linger in the old kirk of St. Bride's, which is surrounded by the sculptured figures of the period that we are here studying. We listen at night to the curfew, and we " people " again with life and with colour the adjoining convent with its stirring memories of exploit, planning and escape. We should not leave Douglas without at least handling the monumental history of *The Douglas-Book*. We shall have time to read the pages that refer to the origins of the riot and contest of the fateful Palm Sunday. If we wish material more briefly penned, we shall find it in a capital little book by the ex-schoolmaster, Mr. C. C. Riach, and in a slighter, but faithful record, *The Church of St. Bride*, by J. D. Hutchison, B.Sc.

At the opening of the novel it is in that old kirk that worship is being held. The English troops then in possession of the castle are met to offer prayer. They are not left to the peace of their observance. For Sir James Douglas and his Scottish soldiers are ready to make the attack to regain the old property and to further the claims of King Robert the Bruce to the throne.

Hazelside may still be visited, where Dickson acted as the accomplice to Douglas in his plot. The dark wood across the hills would provide shelter for the knight as he made his way to the kirk for his deed of slaughter. The opponents who worshipped there were the less prepared for the attack, seeing that the Scottish warriors concealed their armour and swords under the garments of peasants. It was in Sir James, of all his followers, that Bruce had most confidence. To him, on dying, he entrusted the royal heart. When attacked by the Saracens in Spain, on his way to Palestine, Douglas repeated his well-known battle-cry. Holinshed, the chronicler, has this informative sentence : "Though the name and familie of the Douglasses was in some estimation of nobilitie before these daies, yet the rising thereof to honour chanced through this same James Douglas." Barbour, the fourteenth-century poet, also has helped to make the name immortal.

Sir John-de-Walton is loved by a certain Lady Augusta. If he hold the castle for the English for a year and a day, then she has resolved to dower him with her wealth. Clothed as a boy, Augusta goes to Douglasdale in order to make her overtures of maidenly grace to Sir John. In reading a somewhat involved tale such as this, we shall find that this is the golden thread of romance that runs through the texture of the varied happenings, and explains many a passage otherwise difficult to fathom. She is in company with a minstrel called Bertram, who uses as his pretext for his adventure that he wishes to peruse some of the manuscripts of Thomas the Rhymer in the Castle library. He obtains entrance on this plea. In his admission he has won the approval of the sub-governor Aymer. And, as De Walton is suspicious about the

minstrel's presence, this leads to a good deal of
friction between these men of power. Scott shows
a fine analysis of character in his unveiling of the
motives of the disputants. He deems that it is
their pride that prevents them being frank with
one another. It would have put them upon a
common footing if only they had made a disclosure
of their views with honesty and tact. There was
really no just cause for quarrel.

It is when Aymer is sent on his commission
to St. Bride's to interview Augusta, who poses as
a son of Bertram, that he is met by the strange
spectre on the street. Douglas lanes at that time
were protected only by a rude palisade. He rode
through the shifting gleams of moonlight. All
the surroundings readily lent themselves to add
point and reality to his certainty that some un-
wanted warrior had passed him in the night!
He consults Lazarus Powheid about the matter.

Their interview in the sepulchral setting of the
vaults of the old sanctuary is one of the most
arresting scenes in the book. Father Jerome is
at the mercy of the English for every benefit
that he receives. He therefore lays bare to Aymer
the tale of Augusta's residence in St. Bride's, and
she is to be brought forth for trial for conniving
with the minstrel in the seeming plot. But next
morning the room of the supposed son of Bertram
is empty. The prisoner has escaped. None can
offer any clue to the hapless event. How can
Aymer face De-Walton now? How can he explain
the apparent slackness in not immediately bringing
the accused to the bar of justice?

Every reader is intrigued by the romantic and

princely stratagems of Lady Augusta of Berkeley.
It would rob the interest of those readers who have
not yet mastered *Castle Dangerous* if we unfolded
the intricate plot. Ere De-Walton is able to
avail himself of his good fortune, and meet his
intercessor—feud, combat, misunderstanding have
to be overcome.

> " The way is long, my children, long and rough—
> The moors are dreary, and the woods are dark ;
> But he that creeps from cradle on to grave,
> Unskilled save in the velvet course of fortune,
> Hath missed the discipline of noble hearts."

In these words from an old Play, Sir Walter
Scott expresses the sense of mystery and of wise
purpose with which Lady Augusta's path is
bordered. It is enough to say that she (all unknown
to De-Walton) had been working for his
best interests while being threatened with hard-
ships and facing affronts. She was a bene-
factress in disguise, empress of his thoughts,
commander of his actions. Sir Aymer well
describes the difficulty of setting disordered
doings right when he speaks of " unravelling
this tangled skein." The circumstances are
the more involved, as the Earl of Pembroke
has made his famous raid upon the Scottish
troops at Ayr, and the hope of the English
holding Douglas Castle is lost. It is here that
the generous chivalry of the good Sir James is
shown. Fate threw the young heiress into his
hands. He knew that it was for her sake that
De-Walton had been holding the Castle of his
inheritance. Yet, when battle and feud are over,
Douglas graciously absolves the Lady Augusta

from all blame. De-Walton (although he has to leave the Castle) does so with her at his side. If the good Sir James were victor in the struggle, none could ever say that he was unforgiving to his foes. The surrender of Douglas Castle on Sunday 14th March, 1307, stands out in history as a great event. It was the commencement of an era of triumph. Gradually the great part of the Scottish fortresses was handed over. Scott shows how they paved the way for what he calls "the crowning mercy" of Bannockburn. Not only does there open to the reader of *Castle Dangerous* a gloried chapter in the story of our past, but there is also unveiled in vision the promise of a world freed from the ravages of war. The Earl of Home, who owns the present castle, is one of the most ardent champions of the cause of peace. For him, and for all promoters of the League of Nations, there can only be unmixed joy in reflecting on the old sexton, Lazarus Powheid, in St. Bride's. When he heard from Aymer the tale of the spectre on the streets of Douglas, he pointed to the remorseless warfare of the times. Fantastically, and yet with rare insight, he imagined the tormented spirits of the tombs, loitering near these places of contest. These were the "fleshless warriors" who disturb the councils of war. It is no vain fancy! The present great House of Douglas has made it one of its most consecrated tasks to call our land to unstinted effort to interrupt the ravages of war. There is no summons more insistent than from the discontented, "fleshless warriors" who compass us about, and call us to the war for enduring peace.

CHAPTER V

A TEST of a valued book is that we have an amiable envy. We covet the happy task of our friends who as yet have not read it. Such rich enjoyment awaits them, such awakening of romantic hopes lies in store for them on its treasured pages. *Rob Roy* is a tale of adventure, of freebooting, of plots and of villainy, of gentle humour and quiet, pastoral life. Long ago Dr. Macleod of the lone isle of Gigha, who has done so much for Hebridean lore pictured what feast of reason would be possessed when a man made the acquaintance of this book. There is joy in having read *Rob Roy*, if for no other reason, that we are able to introduce the reader to it. There are many, of course, who have mastered it at school or at the University. They, too, will enjoy the remembrance of the hours when they began to love it.

Many of us forecast sunlit tours. Where shall we go ? In our Highland journeys we may wish to linger on the purple moors of Balquhidder to see the last resting-place of Rob Roy himself. We are sure some time to live over again the famous contest in the inn, to image to ourselves the weird figure of Helen Macgregor in her highland fastness, to rehearse anew the sense of the perilous expedition to save a great firm's honour, and to recount the drollery and charm of Bailie Nicol Jarvie. One of Scott's contemporaries was minister at Aberfoyle. His name is the Rev^d. Patrick Graham. He wrote to his friend to tell him that the novelist has an intimate acquaintance with the localities portrayed. This is high testimony from one who was familiar with the land in which the story has its setting. Indeed, few things are more impressive than the artistic manner in which the author weaves the scenery and the actual personnel of his acquaintances into the texture of this novel. No more charming person in the book will be found than Diana Vernon. Scott describes her riding expeditions with rare and vivid portraiture. He admitted that he had been influenced by the sight of Lady Shelley in his description. Writing to his son in 1819, he described her as the boldest horsewoman that he had ever seen. He adds, " I saw her at Paris ride like a lap-wing in the midst of all the aides-de-camp and suite of the Duke of Wellington." It is this intimate contact of the writer of the tales with people that he had met and admired that yields freshness to the portraiture and that relieves it of tedium. The first edition of *Rob Roy* was exhausted in a fortnight. It comprised 10,000 copies. This was the favourite of all the Waverley Novels in the estimate of some men of great literary worth. Lord Rosebery and R. L. Stevenson are two outstanding examples. In one of his essays, Andrew Lang has shown that it gives an excellent survey of the economic conditions of Glasgow in that period. Readers will see the new life of that once quite ordinary Clydeside town opening up and finding its channels of trade with foreign ports.

Scott and the Lure of the Road

" The Saut Market " is by no means a negligible factor in the trade of the period. Mr. Buchan indeed ranks " the Bailie " along with the creations of Molière and Shakespeare. He is a mine of information. He has a droll wit. He is typical of the best in our Scottish race, and if the reader tramp alongside of him from the city, after he has inspected the prison, to his strange haunts in Perthshire, he will come back refreshed and wiser than when he started out.

In the time of Rob Roy there were " mair dirks than Bibles " in the land. Yet the endurance of the man, his loyalty to his friends, his powers of high daring, his desperate purposes, have made him one of the great characters of all time. We never can forget the scene at the water-side when an accomplice cuts the imprisoning belt which bound this dastardly chiel to the horse. We live over again that courageous hour when he slips under the steed's body and plunges into the depths. We see the angry soldiers firing on his supposed moving figure in the water only to find that he had dislodged his plaid and *this* had been their aimless target !

Rashleigh stands with Iago in *Othello* as one of the most repelling types of villainy that art could ever portray. Scott himself must have felt the unholy spell of the man. For the novelist refers to certain poisons which infect the whole well of truth. Rashleigh was in his mind. He goes to every excess of ingenuity to wreck the fortunes of Frank Osbaldistone. He exhibits the most woeful malice to all his rivals ; and even in the last great assault on the Hall, it is as if some fiendish power of enmity and revenge had enthralled his soul.

Rob Roy on His Native Heath

Andrew Fairservice is a masterly picture. He is the type of the old-fashioned gardener. He is cautious almost beyond imagining. He knows a good job when he is in it, and refuses to part with the perquisites that he has, in the hope of large rewards. To use his own quaint language, he will " daiker on wi' the family." He is happy with the supply of his vegetables and fruit, and would be impoverished, he once remarked, if he ever served " a lady who counted the apples." Poor Frank was at his wit's end to know how to tackle him when he induced him to show him the path to the North. Andrew had the faults of a " thrawn " nature. He always had an eye for his own security. With all these flaws he curiously combined a love of pure doctrine, or at least he professed to do so. Scott in his dealings with men very quickly discerned where genuine religion is the really impressive feature of a personality. Where it is a mere veil to conceal defects, no one is more charitable. He has the artist's charm of leaving his creations on the canvas, and of allowing the reader to draw his own conclusions. Sometimes, too, as in the library of Osbaldistone Hall, he allows one of his characters to draw an ironical conclusion which we feel sure is an echo of his own unexpressed view. Dante and other classic authors were being studied by Diana and Frank. The other members of the household were fonder of field sports than of literature. Diana with great insight avers one day that if the folios fell on their heads in the study it would be the only means of making an impression ! This novel is rich in perception of the workings of human nature. It would be difficult to find a story which more deftly paints the happenings that belong to the relation of father to son. Indeed, in the links of interest and of discussion between Frank and his father, there is a glimpse of an autobiography. If we read Lockhart, or any other great Life of Scott, we shall see that the business routine of the office was as unwelcome to young Walter as London was to Frank. It is his son's unwillingness to take a serious part in his business that makes the plot of *Rob Roy* so interesting to youth. The head of the firm is in Holland ; and it is then that the unprincipled nephew finds his opportunity. Lands had been bought in the Highlands. Bills had been given in payment. Rashleigh's transactions had entangled the firm. He had taken away much that was of value. Frank rises nobly to the occasion. He makes an effort to restore his father's credit. This introduces him to the exploits which make so perilous his doings in Rob Roy's countryside.

No reader can pass the scene in Glasgow Cathedral without a sense of awe and enthusiasm. When we visit it, we seem to hear again the summer breeze blow on the trees by the river-side, and hear the rich and sonorous tones of the worshippers as they lift their voices in God's house. If anyone wish a description of a Congregation in its subtle moods and varied attitudes, this scene could not well be excelled. Even more interesting is the tribute that Scott pays to the peerless worth of Scottish worship, its seemly reverence, its deep note of understanding, its simplicity, its sense of the presence of God. The more ornate ritual of continental churches had impressed the author. None could excel in its tender and uplifting decorum and unadorned grace the worship of the Kirk of our fathers.

Truly, there is a well-furnished table awaiting all who yearn to feast from the diet that is here displayed. Here is the study of business-intrigue for those who are planning a life of commerce. Here are the wild and mountainous wastes of isolated regions for the poet and the traveller. There are glowing hours for those who revel in the survey of motives, in the uprising of revolt, in the mastery of good over evil. To some, the workings of the plot may appear a little tardy. Something is gained by Scott's shrewd analysis and by his slowly developing plan. There is no lack of change in the locus of the drama—Bordeaux, London, York, Northumberland, Glasgow, Aberfoyle pass before us. The mere catalogue of places is a faint witness to the broad horizon that sweeps before us, as we travel in Scott's company.

We always seem to come back to " the heathbell of Cheviot," " the blossom of the Border." Readers will remember her confession : " I am a girl and not a young fellow. I would be shut up in a madhouse if I did half the things I have a mind to. . . . I am a plain, true-hearted girl. I dare hardly speak a word for fear of consequences." Much of the plot turns round the doings of Diana—" the Heather-bell of Cheviot." It is acknowledged that she is one of the most successful of Scott's attempts to enter into the understanding of maidenhood. There is a homely vivacity and naturalness about her that win all to her.

CHAPTER VI

GUY MANNERING AND GALLOWAY

In his great book on Scott, published in March of 1932, John Buchan writes of this tale as amongst " the first three." Readers may be able to make up their minds, after the Centenary Year whether *Guy Mannering* may not have claims to be the premier story. There are certainly not a few who, like John Buchan, have a strong regard for this tale. There are many admirers of it who are prepared to advocate it as their favourite.

If we wish to find its dramatic setting, we go to Creetown. This village is one of the secluded places of Galloway. Yet it is worth visiting. It is the Portanferry of Guy Mannering ; and it is on the direct line of Gatehouse-of-Fleet, which claims to be the Kippletringan of the novel. Between these two little towns lies a lovely coastline.

Thomas Carlyle was not easily moved by outward beauty. Yet he placed this stretch of country that separates Creetown from Gatehouse as the fairest walk in Scotland. Queen Victoria seemed to think so too. Perhaps, she was influenced by the sage of Ecclefechan. We question very much whether Carlyle is right in his rapturous praise. It is enough to say that it is one of the most beautiful walks. If we want really to understand *Guy Mannering*, and to read it with intense feeling, we do well to travel the road. There rise up before

us the walls of Ellangowan, as we tread the highway.
Up on the neighbouring hillside we trace the footsteps of Meg Merrilies, " a kind of queen among
the gipsies." Farther on is Dirk Hatteraick's
cave, a place most inaccessible, but which we discovered with the aid of a friendly guide. Out on
the broad sea the imaginative person can well
picture the activities of the smuggling community.
Within sight on a clear day is the Isle of Man.
In those days, shipping was easily procured to the
Isle from this part of the Scottish coast. Indeed,
it provided a quick and easy means to dispatch the
plunder of the desperate men of whom Scott writes.
If any of us can wander along that coast some
summer, and re-create the drama, he will see very
clearly how possible are the happenings of the
book.

What the novelist accomplished was to use the
surroundings, the history, the questionable practices
of the time, the pictures of the background which
so many had ignored, for the purposes of literary
art. It is his genius that amazes us—the genius
that can so interpret these everyday facts, so cast
on them the light of hope, and the shadow
of terror and revolt, that all that is venture-
some becomes ours again as we walk along
the Gatehouse Road. Harry Bertram seems
to look out on us from his playful haunts.
Dominie Sampson, his guardian and tutor stirs
our affectionate interest for his adoring love
for little Harry, and for his absorbing attention
to his beloved books. There is an old mansion not
far from Creetown, Cassencary, where we pause to
have a wistful look at some of the reputed tomes of

Dominie, and to get a glimpse of the once
"prodigious" library. How real this eccentric,
yet lovable man becomes. What learning enriches
his mind. What worlds of beauty and of truth
dazzle his inward sense. We see him sitting
unconcerned on the stair, engrossed in reading,
oblivious to the call of the dinner-bell. We are
delighted at his engaging interest in the growth of
Harry's mind, and of his ingenuous devotion
to Lucy, whom he regards also as his precious
care. The original of the Dominie was a tutor in
the home of Scott at Abbotsford. His patron
vainly tried to get him elected to a charge in the
Church of Scotland. Even in those days, many
congregations were undiscerning in their choice,
and they let this man be "a Stickit Minister"
to the end. He never got the pulpit that he might
have adorned. He has secured an immortal place
amid the figures of literature.

Ere we explore further the treasures of this
book, we may ask : How did Sir Walter gain a
knowledge of the district ? His work as an advocate
of the Court of Session made him an ardent collector
of all kinds of data. In those days advocates pled
in the General Assembly. There was a famous
trial in the Assembly, called the Girthon case.
Scott was the defender of the clergyman at Girthon.
He went down to Galloway to investigate the
circumstances. Much of the local colour, the
aptness of his geographical allusions, the fitness
of his place-names for characters, are due to that
visit of his. We visited Girthon, and Scott appeared
after all these years to be working at our elbow.
We could not but be subdued by the chivalry that

brought him here to say a good word for one who had failed in his sacred task. The Church at Girthon is now in ruins, a beautiful old edifice, with not a few points of interest for the archæologist. If the case were lost in the Assembly, and if this were a blighted Ministry, the advocate was rewarded for his action as a good Samaritan. He brought from the scene of his legal processes the trophies of his growing art. If any truth ought to be engraven on our minds from his expedition, it is his assiduous employment of all resources to enrich the life of that country-side, and to make it a fitting stage for high tragedy. What have we here ? A somewhat bleak country-side in spring-tide, the natural anxiety of the barrister for the success of his " case." None of those hindrances kept him from the flight of fancy. The bread of common life became for him a sacrament.

The story of the lost child, from the days of Homer onwards, has been a recurring one in litera-ture. Scott performs his task with a hand that, in its skill will happily compare with the classic tales. The sense of contrasts, too is very marked in his imaginative painting. Over against the happiness of home and the innocence of boyhood are the malice, the plotting, the almost incredible hatred of the villains in the plot. The quick seizing of Harry by violent men, the rapid passing of the lugger to the unknown seas, the grief of the parent, of Lucy and of Dominie, all are portrayed with the touch of a master. As a man of law, Scott is quick to see the weakness of the impetuous policy of the laird of Ellangowan with the gipsies. How far it led to the tragedy the reader may judge. At all events, the present writer will not easily forget walking down from Derncleuch, and rehearsing the scene of Meg's warning to the laird for his untimely treatment of the gipsies. The smouldering fire on the pass, by the yellow furze, the indignation of this red-cloaked prophetess, the forecast of the decay of his house are certainly memorable items in a marvellous dialogue. We can well understand how someone described Meg Merrilies as " Beelzebub's postmistress." " I was scourged—I was branded," she afterwards confessed. " My resolution lay deeper than scourge or red iron could reach—and now the hour is come ! "

The words which we have last quoted are another instance of the contrasts of the events and figures of the novel. For, this "postmistress of Beelzebub," if she has been the disturbing counsellor of Ellangowan rises in a later scene to the chivalrous championship of the wrongs that afflict his house. It is she in the end who brings the smuggler to his reckoning. In the cause of the old house, which she dearly loves, she loses her life. We must not anticipate too much the glorious *dénouement*. We all know that Harry came to his own, and Meg, in her pride, said that he will be " the best laird that Ellangowan has seen for three hundred years."

In this story there are sufficient incidents to thrill the least sensitive reader. The light and shade that play on the picture help to relieve the more tragic parts of its tension. There is the quiet pastoral countryside, the pleasure of the library, the musical interludes of old-fashioned parties, and the romantic events of hearts stirred by adventure and hope. There is the refreshing talk of the " Gordon arms," which the visitor may still enter to rehearse the doings of the property sale. The prison escape, and the fire, the dim haunts of villainous men, the fierce invective of Glossin in his knavery—all provide food for reverie. If, allied to his love of scenery and romance, the reader has a hankering for justice in a somewhat bewildering world, *Guy Mannering* will provide him with the reasoned sense of equality which guides the narrator in the ups and downs of the plot. There is no pious purpose to put everything right in the end. There is what is a much healthier and truer aim in the novelist—the effort to convince us that we live in a world that is under a rule higher and vaster than our own fashionings. Terror, sorrow, loss, trial weave the texture of our common lot. Yet there is still the golden lustre of love and promise. Evil cannot always sway the hearts of men.

The tale, too, apart from its other features, is worth reading, because of the faith that it stirs in us in the more sombre side of human nature when this is excited to goodness. Virtue, kindliness, chivalry, well up in unexpected places. The worst people have, sometimes, surprising depths of worth in them, if only there be the eye of the artist to reveal these or the glow of the saintly to prompt them to action. There is this marvellous fact also in the passage of the years in a strenuous lifetime. Youth and age are bridged in the strength of sympathy. When Harry comes back after all the anxious years, the Dominie forgets the pathos of the vanished youth. He is willing to begin lessons the next day with his little pupil. *Mary Rose* in J. M. Barrie's play carries with it something of the same delightful allusiveness. Beneath all the fancy there is (both in Barrie and in Scott) this enduring truth—that those who learn and search together are contemporaries. If we start on the pursuit of knowledge, we have begun the quest for perpetual youth.

CHAPTER VII

THE PIRATE——SHETLAND AND ORKNEY

THE very name carries with it the sense of adventure. It is a tale which brings us into a world of Romance in the eighteenth century. It also wafts us to delightful islands where calm and tragedy are strangely blended with stories of the tempest. To appreciate the tale to the full, we sail to Shetland and to Orkney. These are the centres of the plot. We spent unforgettable weeks there to breathe the atmosphere that inspired *The Pirate*. It was when acting as a Lighthouse Commissioner that Scott made the tour. To follow his footsteps is a fascinating pilgrimage. We pass over the Sumburgh Roost, where Captain Cleveland's vessel was wrecked, and where he was rescued by Mordaunt. We tramp over the wide fields from Spiggie to Fitful Head, where Norna, the witch-like dame, cast her spells. We visit that curious rocky nest in the rude arbour where she found her home. We linger by the ruins of Jarlshof Castle, in which Basil Mertoun spent his depressing days. We turn to Scalloway with its memories of wrecks and disasters. We catch glimpses of Tingwall, where the original of Triptolemus fulfilled his Ministry, and also taught an unwilling people the elements of agriculture. We image to ourselves the kind of house that Burgha Westra hosts presented to their guests in welcome feast and revel. We weave pictures of Magnus Troil in his jovial hospitality. We find fascinating contrasts in the temperaments of Minna and Brenda. Minna is a girl of reflective outlook. Brenda is more joyous, and less concerned by the weight of her burden. How real Scott makes them in their converse and recreations. How easy to re-create them to our fancy, as we see the more sporting lass climbing the heights, the meeker maiden courting less daring pleasures, holding companionship with the sea in its quieter moods.

We advocate the actual sight of the scenes that suggested to the novelist his stirring plots. To dwell in Shetland is to live over again the earlier scenes of *The Pirate*. We share the comradeship of the Captain, as he enjoys his gladsome friendships. We are mastered by the music of their merriment. We share the dreams that the girls fashion to their untried hearts of the great world of peril and of hope that lies beyond the narrow limits of their island-home. Have not Cleveland and Mordaunt broken the spell for them? Is not their unrest, their quickening hope and fear, the beginning for them also of a great venture? The isle has that light and shade that suggest mystery. Its peaceful crofts, its long stretches of moorland, its quiet, meditative people, its rich sunsets, its pasture-lands give the feeling of colour and life which make the background possible. This is the kind of unexpected setting where a pirate might be found holding his listeners enthralled, as he tells of his voyages on the high seas or his enforced exile on some strange outpost of Empire. Little wonder that he comes as the magnet, and also as the herald of revolt. Leisurely homes are no longer at peace. Magistrates are busy in tracking his crimes. The rival in love has little chance to resist his villainy. Norna of the Fitful Head is ever on the alert to watch his desperate doings, to quell the riot that his coming presages, and to temper the fears of those whose future fate hangs in the balance.

Possibly the desperate happenings might prove too exciting a thrill were it not that the book is relieved by flashes of real humour. At Stourburgh we are in the refreshing company of Yellowley, the graduate of St. Andrews. We also listen submissively to the strictures of Barbara, that droll and economical sister of his. Little escapes her vigilant eye, and very little is disbursed needlessly from her purse. Her larder is not too well stored, and she guards it with frugal and unkindly concern.

Part of the interest of the tale is sustained by the disappearance of Mordaunt. His father learns that Norna may know something of his doings. Every reader of *The Pirate* finds food for awesome reverie by the Kirk of St. Ringan's as the interview takes place. Critics have pointed out that Norna is a creation of pure imagination, whereas other weird figures in various novels have had some basis in history. These instances are Magdalene Graeme in *The Abbot*, Meg Merrilies in *Guy Mannering*, and the White Lady of Avenel in *The Monastery*. Norna is different from all these.

In our southward voyage from Shetland, it is natural to touch at Orkney. If then the reader of this novel linger over the pages that describe Troil's party on St. John's Eve, it will make more vivid for him the scene if he sail to Kirkwall. For it is to that town that the scene changes. Mordaunt is wounded by Cleveland. The victim is taken to Hoy, which the traveller sees rising from the mist like a giant of the night awaking from his sleep. The assailer goes to Kirkwall to join his consort-vessel. It is here that the Captain has his encounter with Bryce Snailsfoot. Here comes the discovery of the stolen clothes, the clever ruse of Bryce to involve Cleveland in criminal action, the heroic rescue by the pirates, and the triumphant escape from the harbour-mouth. The scene of the fight is a very vivid one. Scott is in his element when he paints the faces of these bronzed sailors who bear the marks of their tropical journeys. None but will revel in the sight of the cutlasses and pistols. No just person but will rejoice in the overthrow of Snailsfoot's plans and the discovery of his trickery. It was Shakespeare who described pirates as " water-thieves," and yet, proverbially, their untutored honour is revealed, and their gallant championship of their comrade, in this book that discloses all falsity.

One of the most striking scenes is enacted within the precincts of the old Cathedral. The visitor wanders round this fine old structure which has been unharmed by the inroads of the Reformation. He pictures the hour when Cleveland meets Minna. These ancient walls seem to have witnessed hapless sights ; and the echoes of the voices of the lovers are with us, as we image to ourselves these figures of Scott's fine, creative art. We do not like to use pedantic words in describing the art of the novelist. Yet they are apt enough when all others escape us. It is the *fecundity* of Scott that impresses the reader. A brief visit by the Wizard of the North to those enchanting isles, and then by Sir Walter's power of constructive genius there is produced this stirring tale. We are in the hands of a magician who makes unexpected deeds shine out before us and sets a romantic light on the doings of adventurers.

Yet, with it all, there is a pathos in the closing tragedy. Minna feels that she has been deluded. She had pictured the hero of her dreams as a being girt with impossible virtues. Now he is revealed in his true guise. Scott shows how a woman of insight can pierce through all insincerity. Then, as we tarry with her and her lover under the shadow of the Stennis Stones, something of the curious sense of the majesty of human life and the mystery of broken and disappointed friendship is enhanced by the wonder of Nature around. As we walk out from Stromness to these Stennis blocks of un-explained masonry, as we look out towards the sea, all the picture seems to blend with the terror and faltering hope in the hearts of the actors. The chivalry of Mordaunt in his desire to save Minna from desperate hands, the determined purpose of Bunce to place Cleveland beyond the reach of villainy, the burning vessel in the bay, and the fateful gaze of the prisoners towards the Halcyon are all described with dramatic art.

What, then, are some of the direct gains of reading *The Pirate*? There is the immediate contact with the life of the island, its manners and thought. The delightful commingling of Norse ideas, the familiarity with Norse expressions give the reader a feeling of being on foreign shores, and yet amongst hospitable people. Especially if he visits Shetland will he appreciate the new lingua. There is a breeziness and homeliness in their habits, and withal a thoughtfulness and interest in reading, that will act as a mental tonic to him. Another asset is that this novel with its variety of character makes us more convinced than ever how complex is the study of the human mind. Those who are lovers of Milton will find in Minna and Brenda, *Il Penseroso* and *L'Allegro* happily presented. They are together under one roof—members of the same family. They are (like so many sisters) moulded to different patterns. Cleveland is to all appearance the picture of a chivalrous knight. How slowly his real outlook is unveiled! Triptolemus is born before his time, far in advance of his parish in knowledge of agriculture. It is only when his work is done that it is realised that he has been an unrecognised pioneer of labour. Who would have imagined Vaughan as the unacknowledged father of Cleveland? What must have been the feelings of the proprietor of Jarlshof when he sees stamped upon the life of the Pirate the habits of desperate bravado that he taught him long ago?

We cannot leave the book without marking a further gain. It is the mellowing of Norna's strong and superstitious nature to a more spiritual simplicity. She has woven many spells. She has surveyed hazardous undertakings. She has seen tragedy, and averted sorrow. She has played her part as the supposed mistress of the ocean. Now she grows trustful of Him who holds the waves and the winds in the hollow of His hand.

CHAPTER VIII

THE advantage of being drawn to literature rather
than coerced is that it becomes our own choice.
Ruskin was most emphatic in the place of some such
reasonable selective process in the development of
literary taste. He favoured the happy entrance of a
reader into a library where the great departments of
literary lore were sufficiently evident to entice the
eye and the heart. When we light on some work in
fiction, drama, or poetry, our willing choice makes
more possible a ready reception of its contents.
We are drawn to it. We capture its treasure. We
learn to make it our own because we learn to love it.

If this method were more common, then *The
Antiquary* for a good many people would prove
quite irresistible. We are in the midst of a Scottish
fishing community as the tale proceeds. A quaint
vendor exclaims, " It's no fish ye're buyin', it's men's
lives." A sentence such as this at once convinces
us of the need to sojourn by that seaport of Auchmithie, which lies a few miles from Arbroath.
Scott visited it for the atmosphere of the place.
When we see the old customs of the village life, as
they are presented in pictures of the period, and
when we pass the homes of the people, very similar
to what they were when *The Antiquary* was written,
it is as if the book presented in a living pageant

deeds which appear as real as if they had happened yesterday. "The beach," says Sir Walter, "was a neutral field where even a justice of peace and a strolling mendicant might meet upon terms of mutual forbearance." The tale owes much to the uneven coast where it has its locus. The rugged, precipitous promontories, the stately Abbey of Aberbrothock are all part of the texture of the narrative. It is undeniably a tale which traces to the sea much of its tragical appeal, with all the mystery of that wide expanse, and the tempests that break upon the wild shore. Scott was a close student of Shakespeare. Quotations from the plays seem to leap to his mind with an enviable aptness. He lets us hear the music of the words of a great drama. They are like the whisper of the winds on the ocean that he loved :

> "There is a cliff whose high and bending head
> Looks fearfully on the confined deep ;
> Bring me but to the very brim of it,
> And I'll repair the misery thou dost bear."

This verse from *King Lear* is a witness to the close alliance between a tale and its environs. It gives us in a few lines a glimpse of the kind of scenic effect that the author has in view, and it carries us also to the very theme round which this later drama has its setting. It is when brave souls are brought " to the brim " of the cliffs, as we shall discover, that misery in one of its worst forms is "repaired." It is poor criticism of the novelist to find fault that he mentions sands at Auchmithie—and we search for them there in vain. The test of the authentic worth of an artist does not lie in his absolute fidelity to every detail, rather in his power to make real the great happenings. He shews us a wide horizon. He makes us feel at home and in touch with the main features when we tread the ground over which his fancy travelled. Sands or no sands, the village of Auchmithie becomes a place of intimate and picturesque suggestiveness when we see one of its figures as described by Scott :—" A middle-aged woman with a face which had defied a thousand storms sat mending a net at the door of one of the cottages. A handkerchief, close-bound about her head, and a coat which had formerly been a man's gave her a masculine air, which was increased by her strength, uncommon stature, and high voice. ' What are ye for the day, your honour,' she screamed to Oldbuck ; ' caller haddocks and whitings, a bannock fluke, and a cock-padle ? ' " If added vividness to the scene is needed, it is found in the reference to the Bell Rock, which was a peril to mariners, and which was known to all fishermen on the coast. Scenes such as these are rendered more striking by the swiftness with which our many-sided novelist transports his readers to places hallowed and serene. St. Ruth's Abbey is undisturbed by the strident tones of these cries. It carries with it a serenity all the more marked by contrast.

" Of seats they tell where priests, 'mid tapers dim,
  Breathed the warm prayer or tuned the mid-night hymn ;
  To scenes like these, the fainting soul retired,
  Revenge and anger in these cells expired :
  By Pity soothed, Remorse lost half her fears,
  And softened Pride dropped penitential tears."

There can be little doubt that the villainy of

Dousterswivel seems the more heinous in the reader's judgment because of the clever touch of this literary artist in setting his plot amid this old shrine. The history of the Abbey, its saintly vigils, its witness to things unseen, in the centuries, become the background for deeds of crime. In the sacred surroundings, the base planning and deceit of the adventurer come more quickly under the condemnation of the spectator. Not that evil is more readily condoned, if performed outside a temple. The skill of the painter is seen in portraying an attempted act of deception within sight of the altar. There are in the book also apt allusions to old customs of the neighbourhood and some eccentricities. In those days the post-office of Fairport was the centre of a group of villagers of whom Mrs. Mailsetter, the post-mistress was a leading light. They were able very freely to discuss the doings of the neighbourhood from what they had learned from their recent mails. Scott is never more sparkling with wit than when he introduces us to their conversation.

There are side lights too on the somewhat lethargic moods of the seafaring men. On the hard-working women much of the burden fell. Jenny indignantly protests—" As sune as the keel o' the coble touches the sand, deil a bit mair will the lazy loons work, but the wives kilt their coats, and wade into the surf to tak' the fish ashore." It is a fascinating study, with light and shadow in the picture. Every mile of the surrounding countryside is fraught with literary interest. So deeply has the tale haunted the place, that the chief actors appear, as we visit their surroundings, to be our own familiar friends. The people of Arbroath are still deeply interested in the novel that has added to the fame of their good old town. We are brought once and again to marvel at the genius that so skilfully wed this tale to the setting that Nature has obviously provided for it. No part of the British Isles fits it so well. There is a splendour about the scenery that has cast its radiance on the pages. The people move naturally. The resources of the district are a passport to the understanding of the plot. It is easy to admire it when the literary feat is accomplished. To perform the task when travelling was at a minimum, compared to the present vogue, makes the writing of the book more admirable.

> " So sinks the day star in the ocean bed,
>   And yet anon repairs his drooping head."

To see the setting sun is to enter into the sense of the idyllic. To find in light and sea and simple folk the birthplace of love, laughter and tragedy, is the token of an author's regal worth. Despite all his severest critics say, it entitles him to immortality. It would be, of course, quite impossible to tell the whole story. We rather attempt to paint some of its alluring features. Why should we buy it ? Or, if we already possess it, why should we take it down from its high shelf in our library ? The first inducement is that its scenes are laid in two of the most famous counties of Scotland— Midlothian and Forfarshire. It is not a long journey from Edinburgh to the Hawes Inn in Queensferry. The place is still standing, and when we went there we could readily picture the meeting of Mr. Oldbuck with Mr. Lovel. Oldbuck is the Antiquary of the tale. We went north to see the old house in Forfarshire where his "original" is supposed to have had his home. It is quite like the place where such a man would love to stay. It is full of great paintings and old curios. Mr. Oldbuck often walked into Fairport from Hospitalfield; and Scott called his home Monkbarns. How real and alive are his character, his contests with his sister, his conflicts with the clergyman, Mr. Blattergowl, his feuds with Sir Arthur Wardour, his constant ridicule of his nephew. To him the things of the past are almost more important than those of the present. Nothing delights him more than to reconstruct some forgotten scene in history, or to dissect the interminable theories which gather about an ancient site. Withal, he is an appealing personality. He is moved on occasion to sorrow, and he befriends the poor.

It was over a warm dispute with his neighbour, Sir Arthur, that something of a tragedy had its rise. They could not come to agreement as they sat arguing at a dinner-party. The result was that Sir Arthur left the table in high disdain, and on the way home he and his daughter, Lucy, were overtaken by a storm. It was one of the most terrific that has raged along that coast. Monkbarns is only a few miles from Arbroath. This town is the "Fairport" of the novel. Readers may form some idea of the coast if they travel by the Aberdeen train south from Montrose, and gain the contour of the seaboard passing Lunan Bay. We walked one afternoon along the sands to Red Head. We looked out at that angry ocean. We pictured to ourselves these fearful happenings, the wild tempest of that memorable night and the rescue by Edie Ochiltree, Lovel, and their friends. The scene readily recurs to memory. Imagination makes it live before us. Let every reader make these great happenings his mental possession as he reads *The Antiquary*. He will there learn how great is the magnitude of Nature, as man in his helplessness is flung against it. He will also discover that the immensity of storms and all dim forces may be controlled by the hand of God. He will find also that he rises from the survey of these thrilling events with an extraordinary confidence in human nature. In these hours of rescue, classes, hitherto divided, are brought together. All ranks are levelled before the Highest. The rich forgets his disdain, for he is subject to equal perils. The poor do not recollect their animosity, for it is their province to help. Edie and his comrades are willing to hazard their lives even for a hated house-owner. Love brings them together at the feet of God.

There is space in this brief chapter to refer to another exciting section of the tale. It is that which pictures the remorse of Lady Glenallan's servant. We shall have to study the book at leisure in order to learn of the wrong that had been done to an innocent victim, and how her maid aided and abetted her. We shall find the bitter happenings rehearsed. They are described in the manner that Shakespeare employs in some of the finest of his plays. This comes in old age and on the eve of death, in the awakening in the Bedlam of the voice of conscience, and the pain which attends an unpardoned sin. There are great works of literature which show to us the evil effects of wrong done to others, e.g., the Fifty-First *Psalm*, *Macbeth*, Coleridge's *Ancient Mariner* and *The Scarlet Letter*. Few descriptions can easily excel the shadowed hours which overwhelm old Elspeth as she mourns over the past. Scott is at his greatest when he analyses the human heart and when he reveals its depth. He is also a true artist. He has always light as well as shade in his picture. The ending of the tale reveals the promise and the gladness in which the sorrowful events leap to promise. Wrongs are righted and the lawful heir is restored. If our readers desire to find the proper stage on which to let the figures of *The Antiquary* walk to and fro, they must wend their way to Auchmithie, that there they may weave the background of the Mucklebackits' home. We sailed right along the coast, past the weird caves and crags to Aberbrothick. We re-created the drama which has its setting in the ruins of the old Abbey. Dousterswivel creeps out again in his villainy from that fine old sanctuary. We see the plots and the plannings of that ill-disposed German, and we taste again something of the humour and the awe in which Scott makes his figures meet their victim on the memorable night of the assault.

The story, too, is relieved by passages of rare tenderness, of infinite human interest. We cannot but learn to love the characters of the tale. In the appealing guise of intrigue and romance, of sorrow and of sport, we find that our kinship with them is made one. Saintsbury, in his *Elizabethan Literature*, has told us how the power to paint a perennial type is the mark of a genius. Anyone can sketch the life of the exceptional, the abnormal. To make men and women live and think and act in such a way that we are holding up a mirror to humanity as it lives throughout the ages, *this* is the mark of a real artist. We introduce readers to different ages and to varied heroes and heroines. These, we trust, make history live before them. We glean something of the harvest of Scott's profound knowledge of life, his innate sense of justice. We are attracted to him, not only as an author but as a man. If those who follow these discussions have time to peruse Lockhart's great *Life of the Wizard of the North*, much light will be shed upon each novel as we survey it. We shall see the workings of his own experience, the growing power of his craftsmanship. The years that follow the Centenary shall be the entrance for many of us into a Palace of Beauty, where we shall wish to linger, to enrich our own minds, and to make life more gladsome for others.

CHAPTER IX

THE HEART OF MIDLOTHIAN

IT is often asked whether the novel can well be dramatised without injury to its movement. Attempts have been recently renewed to do so, and this tale is one of the favourites for such treatment. It is worth making reference to this. For if the reader has studied the writings, as they come from the pen of Sir Walter, the stage-setting is the means of adding conviction to his mind that local colouring has much to do with the true delineation of the characters. We find ourselves here in the county which has given its name to the title. The Scottish Capital is a picturesque scene for the visualising of an era in the Eighteenth century. The opening acts gather round the old historic Tolbooth. The Porteous riots were a source of disturbance to the city. News of the disorder had reached London. With a measure of anxiety King George II heard of the unpleasing happenings. Porteous had gone beyond the law in his treatment of some of the disturbers. It was his reprieve after the sentence of death had been passed on him that roused the spirit of revenge. The Edinburgh mob of the period is reputed to have been one of the fiercest in Europe. Geordie Robertson was one of the leaders in this revolt. His action in leading Porteous to his fatal hour of doom was one of the sensational tragedies of an exciting era. The effort on a dark, eventful

night to find some clue to the mystery brought
Reuben Butler to haunt the weird path that leads
past the Salisbury Crags. An old song echoes the
words:

> " Arthur's seat shall be my bed,
> The seat shall ne'er be pressed by me,
> St. Anton's well shall be my drink,
> Sin' my true love's forsaken me."

These imposing ridges are easily remembered by
visitors to the city. Scott shows his power of
artistic contrast by bringing the shadowed events
which herald his tale alongside of the peaceful
dwelling of Davie Deans. The picture should be
given from Scott's own canvas. " The prospect,
in its general outline, commands a close-built, high-
piled city, stretching itself out beneath in a form
which, to a romantic imagination, may be supposed
to represent that of a dragon ; now, a noble arm
of the sea, with its rocks, isles, distant shores and
boundary of mountains ; and now a fair and fertile
champaign of country, varied with hill, dale and
rock, and skirted by the picturesque ridge of the
Pentland mountains. As the path gently circles
around the base of the cliffs, the prospect, composed
as it is of these enchanting and sublime objects,
changes at every step and presents them blended
with, or divided from, each other in every possible
variety which can gratify the eye and the imagination.
When a piece of scenery so beautiful, yet so varied—
so exciting by its intricacy, and yet so sublime—is
lighted up by the tints of morning or evening, and
displays all that variety of shadowy depth, exchanged
with partial brilliancy, which gives character even

to the tamest of landscapes, the effect approaches near to enchantment." Scott, with his fondness for attaching certain figures in his tale to places, makes the abode of Deans at St. Leonard's Crags. It lies between Edinburgh and Arthur's Seat. It adjoins the King's park.

Until Robertson had anything to do with Effie their cottage is one of the happiest in the vale. Davie is a douce Presbyterian, somewhat stern, but the example of a strict orthodoxy and an unblemished life. In the realm of thought that era was a somewhat rigid school of morality and reasoned analysis. Evangelicalism in its warmer aspects was not so distinct a characteristic of religion as was the rigid, authoritative adherence to rule. It is possible that the moral lapse in this home was partly the reflex of a somewhat unsympathetic restraint. Effie fell. We cannot read the story without feeling that the onus of it all did not entirely lie with her.

The peaceful board, with its gay company, at St. Leonard's Crags is disturbed by the officers of law. Effie is accused of a crime that she has not committed. The setting of the plot in the midst of a locale intertwined with the tradition of a high ethic, adds to the blight of that disordered garden of the soul. It is one of the extraordinary features of Scott's genius that his atmosphere is sensed with such careful choice. " The Lily of St. Leonard's," as Effie is called, evokes all the deeper sense of pathos in that her fall is set over against the background of Puritanism. Unhappily, too, there was a disposition in the eighteenth century to imagine that one error, grave as it may be, is only the precursor of a deeper sin. Effie suffered from that suspicious survey of her movements. If the historian will run parallel lines alongside of the domestic life of that era, he will be surprised to find how accurately Scott enters into the particular mental mood. This is more than mere scenic effect. Yet is it not the case that geographical and natural conditions often only anticipate for us the moral attributes ? It would be fatalistic to regard the one as in any way justifying the other. No man is conditioned by his surroundings. Edinburgh and its rugged setting, the long story of its feuds and defences, put grit into the soul of men such as Davie Deans. Their mood does not dispose them to charity. When we see his daughter, Jeanie, at Muschat's Cairn, then is not Nature in her ruggedness a replica of that stern spirit which recognises right from wrong ? In the interview Geordie Robertson seems to compel Jeanie to be loyal to the interests of her sister—even if she wander from the rigid truth. She has not lived for naught under the shadow of these hills. They have often echoed for her the commandments of Sinai. They do not explain the nobility of an ethical standard, but they are at least weaved into Scott's thought. As an Edinburgh boy, he had shared that upbringing. As he passed the Castle Rock to the High School, he imbued the strict teaching of undeviating loyalty to conscience. He was unconsciously preparing himself to be the interpreter of Jeanie's soul. That unrelenting submission is no monopoly of any nation. It is not unfair to the traditions of other races to suggest that the British norm has something in it which is worthy to be laid alongside the Judaic witness to righteousness. In the prison, at the Tolbooth, Effie cannot understand her sister's refusal to speak the word that would save her. Nothing can excel in its moving impulse the unspeakable love of the girl who after the trial starts forth and accomplishes the journey to London on Effie's behalf. How much the pictorial drapery of the locale helps the progress of the drama—the pastoral quiet of Liberton, the bells of St. Giles' Cathedral tolling the hour of doom, the beauteous English lanes that she travelled foot-sore and weary. To reach her destination that long road which divides Edinburgh from London had to be travelled. It might readily, of course, be argued that any spot is fitted to be the highway on which footpads seek to carry out their nefarious work. Yet here again, wherever the attack took place on Jeanie by Tyburn Tam and his accomplices, the isolation of the surroundings is well described. Scott's knowledge of the conditions of travel in 1737 helps him to make vivid the scene. He shows how infrequent was the intercourse between the two cities. He mentions as a proof of this that even in his day men still remembered that upon one occasion the mail from London arrived in Edinburgh with only one letter in it. She was within walking distance of Grantham and exclaimed :—" I'm glad to hear there's a hill. For baith my sicht and my very feet are weary o' sic tracts of level ground—it looks a' the way between this and York, as if a' the land had been trenched and levelled, whilk is very wearisome to my Scotch een. When I lost sicht of a muckle blue hill ca'd Inglebors, I thought I hadna' a friend left in this strange land." She had conscience for her guide. When overtaken, and beset, it is suggestive to find that a moment of leisure gave her time to reflect on travellers along as dusty a road in Palestine, who found heart of grace in an old Hebrew lyric. It is with delight that Scott brings her to freedom, to the sight of thatched roofs and blue smoke rising from them. Like the shepherd boy in Bunyan, she carried in her heart the herb called heartsease. Part of her joy was in the sight of a Church. The author looked on these Gothic edifices as the most reverential places that are to be found in Christendom. Surely none save one with the æsthetic instincts of this novelist could bring the reader so naturally from the terror of the highwaymen's threats to the peace of the shrine. He does not argue about the events. He sees them, in the rich colouring of England's pleasant countryside, and in the fancy of his brain. The idyllic pastoral beauty makes more poignant the terror of the scenes which precede. For Madge Wildfire has been relegated to the sore and secret sufferings of her heart by Geordie Robertson. Effie has taken Madge's place of privilege. Nothing short of a Providence has rescued Jeanie, her defender, from her foes. She views Queen Caroline and lays her request before her. Dean Stanley paid a glowing tribute to Her Majesty and the enrichment she gave to the Court of her time. Is there not more than artistic skill in bringing Jeanie into her presence ? The simple maid's reminder of the worth of little kindnesses, of which she spoke to the Queen, lingers in the memory. If her speech reach the heart, it is not because the spiritual teaching is quite original. It is partly because queen and suppliant are woven together into one texture of beauty, with a kinship of spirit which seems the more engaging because it is the reflection of the loveliness of earth.

Those who have visited Richmond will be able to sympathise more readily with the feelings of the heroine when ushered into the presence of the Queen. The park had long been the favourite home of Queen Caroline. It was during the absence of George II on the Continent in 1736 that the Porteous riots referred to had taken place. On his return, Jeanie could not have a more sagacious advocate than the Queen to plead her cause. It was said of her, " she loved the real possession of power rather than the show of it." She had been displeased by the severe measures that the Duke of Argyle had offered against Edinburgh after the Revolt. It is to her enduring honour that she did not permit the strained relations that existed between her and the Duke to act as a barrier to his overtures in defence of Effie Deans. Sir Walter shows himself the master of apposite phrase and of truly appropriate local setting in the interview. The whole narrative is burdened with a sense of tension in which great happenings have their rise. Who shall say that Scott was not an artist ? Who without the painter's skill could so finely bring Jeanie from the perils of the roadway to her audience of the King ? How simply and tersely the meeting is portrayed.

In all the tortuous path of her sacrificial devotion, Jeanie comes bearing in her memory the fragrance of the roads that she has passed, the scent of the gardens, but also the sense of weariness. If she refused to utter in the Law Court at Edinburgh the one word that would have saved her sister, she won

her freedom with the offering of a more costly gift—
her devoted love. The great Elizabethan poet makes
the challenge :

> " Lord, who would live turmoiled in a court,
>   And may enjoy such quiet walks as these ? "

Walk and tragedy and soul are so intertwined
as to be indeed a trinity of treasures. We cannot
separate the maid from her journey. We cannot
dissociate the drama from its surroundings. From
each spot en route there seems to rise the sense of
something spiritual. It is as if here we are in the
midst of two contending forces. There are moments
in life when the stages in a pilgrimage are milestones
upon a way that leads us beyond our own striving.
It is within our power, with *The Heart of Midlothian*
and a map as our companions, " to enjoy such quiet
walks as these."

CHAPTER X

IS ROMANTICISM INTERWEAVED WITH RELIGIOUS FEELING IN THE WAVERLEY NOVELS?

WE have come to a moment of pause on our journey with Scott through some of his outstanding tales. We propose now to ask the reader to explore with us a question which must have met him often in his study of the Wizard of the North. If Scott starts us on a pilgrimage, he seems to have in view (however implicitly) a larger adventure,—the pathway of life. He has made a real contribution to the study of human nature. Has he not done more? Does he not yield to his devotees a truer sense of the inward meaning of this complicated Universe? Is he not much more than a story-teller? May he not be in the truest sense a spiritual guide?

In the second part of the Volume we propose to introduce our readers to some added charms in other conspicuous novels. This breathing-space at our half-way house may be to us a retrospect as well as a prospect. The interlude may have this advantage in providing us with a working Philosophy of Scott's attitude towards ethical questions. It may help us to link him in thought to some of the wisest teachers of his age. It has been said by a great English critic that " Scott was intellectually fast-rooted in the Eighteenth Century—the last and greatest of the race of realists who created the English novel." This is true. The emphasis on

Romanticism in the Waverley Novels

it in works of literature is apt to obliterate from our minds as distinctive a phase of his genius. He was not in the strictest sense an initiator of abstruse thought. Yet he was in touch with contemporary studies and life in the highest circles in the University, and amongst the men of letters of his day. He was an omnivorous reader. We are sometimes inclined to forget the intellectual and poetic age in which he lived. His friendship with Southey, Wordsworth and Crabbe is a symptom of this. He struck the most authentic note as a Romanticist. Was he not also a revealer of truth ? It is this aspect of his work which does not fully secure the justice which is its due. It would be unfortunate if this decade of reviving interest in the Waverley Novels failed fully to adjudge the work that Scott did as a sagacious thinker. He did not set out to edify people. May it not be that he did it the more effectively on this account ? He was not an official representative of Religion. Does not his minute knowledge of the Bible scintillate throughout his works ? Is there not a tenfold value in the phrase or allusion to sacred truth because these stand forth, illumined by some actual condition in the world of romance or of history that he has described ?

Matthew Arnold declared that 1832 is a real epoch in literature. *His view is that the death of Sir Walter Scott marks the end of one era and the beginning of another*. The verdict has never seriously been denied. Professor Moffatt writes, " It is half a century since this was written, and Arnold's judgment still holds good." When we touch this life, we are wafted to a less material world. We reach the realm of Idealism. Idealism, as a recent philosopher has wisely said, " affirms what is *spiritual* as sole reality." Dr. Hale Amos, a Cambridge scholar, has gone out of his way to comment critically on Sir Walter. It is on the ground, strangely enough, of this Idealistic view of the past. Particularly, does Dr. Amos blame him for his seeming bias, as he pictures the mediæval world. In the view of this writer, Scott misconstructed that era. He made men imagine that it was far nearer the standard of the New Testament than sober history will allow. Indeed, he feels that it was partly due to the halo cast on the Church that the Oxford Movement had its rise.

The issue which this student raises is too wide to discuss fully in this Essay. Let it be said that the Idealism complained of is surely one of the alluring qualities of a real teacher. It is part of his constructive art. Minds such as Newman and Keble were enticed to see hidden values in a neglected period. Not alone of the ritual of the Middle Ages, but of the simplest forms of Post-Reformation services on the Scottish hillside, Sir Walter is equally appreciative.

If we are to know the past, is it not as needful that we should learn its richest triumphs as well as its unpleasing features ? When we come to think of it, no period since the Apostolic Age has ever quite imaged the standard of the New Testament. The wisdom of the Idealist is witnessed in the case of Scott. By abstracting what is noblest, does he not prove his right to teach us ? Does he not bring us nearer to one phase of reality ? A discriminating thinker expresses it well when he suggests that if Scott has not described the mediæval period as it is, he has done so as we would like it to be. In the scope of his historical novels he surveys seven centuries of struggle. Men who have won high place in history at Oxford and Cambridge admit the worth of this idealism. They see in it an authenticating note. The reasonable view is that Scott has created the needful atmosphere. In so doing he has given an impulse to the understanding of history as strong as the unvarnished record of facts. Professor Mackie, of Glasgow University, has given powerful testimony to this fact. Of course, we may ask, is all this verified? Old castles, tournaments, deeds of chivalry, modes of living, acts of worship, may not have been always as ethereal as painted by the Wizard. True, but all the time he is imparting instruction. For in his hands what is enduring is rescued from neglected archives. To be brought even for an hour to gain a glimpse of the idyllic is to see time in a new significance,—*sub specie eternitatis.*

Besides, this rôle of moral instruction, unconscious as it was, was the more necessary. The Century which preceded Arnold's " real epoch " was one of a sceptical outlook. In Bishop Butler's time, no man seemed less reasonable if he cast his jest at Religion. Hume had made more feasible an adverse attitude to faith. Locke had induced a certain mechanism in his survey of impressions. The spiritual world seemed more unreal. Long before, there was a feeling of unrest in thinking minds. G. K. Chesterton goes so far as to say that the Seventeenth Century ended with a mark of interrogation. He wittily compares this with the little crooked figure of Alexander Pope. *He* carried even in his contorted form the question mark of men of culture.

Now, here was part of Scott's service as a teacher. Many were not able to follow the teaching of Berkeley. He did for the people something of the enlightening work of that great reasoner. He convinced men that the world around us is not a substance of permanence. He moulded distant eras. He bridged time and space. At his imaginative touch, figures nothing short of heroic leapt out of forgotten crevices. In one of his Essays, Andrew Lang shows that Scott at his best reaches the level of Greek tragedy. Now, to do so is surely a spiritual art. Creative work, dramatic situations bring us beyond the sense of what is seen and temporal. He who can analyse motives, who can pierce beneath all appearance to the inner workings of the mind is a real preceptor. If we depict man at his highest, or at his worst, in the act we posit the sense of his need of God. We assume *per se* the function of the seer. In the discussion which this Volume elicits, it may be well asked : Is this not a greater service to mankind than that of the unerring historian ?

On the pages of Scott there is a parallel to what happens in the Fourth Gospel. The thing is so fragrant, so unsubstantial—we pause and ask : Have we not here something *more* than history ? An event does not gain its full meaning merely by having happened. When recovered from the mists of antiquity, does it not acquire something which it never had before ? Is it not part of the artist's craft to set it in an enduring pageant ? Does it not rise above the things of time and sense ? It belongs to the genius of Scott that he does this. Augustine Birrell, Bagehot and a host of critics acknowledge the debt that we owe. There are classic eras that occur to everyone. The master light is cast on our common life. Scenes rehearsed in this volume occur to the reader—the meeting of Meg Merrilies with the Laird when the gipsies have been evicted, the disclosure of the villainy of Leicester, the picture of the wisest fool in Christendom in the *Fortunes of Nigel*, the weird hours of darkness by the Stennis Stones in *The Pirate*. He is teaching us at every turn. It may be done not less effectually, if, in his prophetic language, there be no " Thus saith the Lord." God speaks when the conscience and the heart respond. His is not a dictum *ab extra* only, but a voice within. Karl Barth does not expound this aspect of Revelation. Yet every reader of Scott feels the still, small voice.

We may probe even deeper, and ask : " What is Scott's religion ? " This would require a lengthy chapter to itself. We can only summarise. It is a faith of acceptance, not of theological analysis. The problems that harass the psychologist in his study do not exist for him. His faith is primarily not one of thought, but of action. Possibly, his military training partly accounts for this. If he had read philosophy more widely, he would have been at home with Kant's categorical imperative. In the Calendar of Saints he might stand for Wordsworth's *Happy Warrior*. Sometimes we weave fancies of him as our St. Francis of Assisi. True, he did not call Poverty his Sister. But he went out on a world-wide mission as important.

He lavishly laid his gift on the altar. He was always busy. He had a mystic sense of beauty. He revelled in God's fair universe. He had the captivating instinct of St. Francis in stirring undreamt of good in the most debased. We may recall Tom Purdie in the Sheriff Court of Selkirk. Scott served the Lord with the gaiety of a little child, and the glowing assurance of the devout.

Thus, poet and novelist earn their right to educate. For in the Miltonic sense he was a good man. From king to peasant man felt the spell. This was the secret of his charm. He might not have felt quite easy in the questions that men discuss in scholarly conclaves. Had he taken part, all would have risen to their feet and called him Master. This engaging power of his has been unveiled by Hugh Walpole in his edition of *The Letters* of the friends of Scott.

He had this advantage over others in professional life. He was not an official counsellor. He could pursue the art of instructor more by implication than by direct statement. " A verse finds him whom a sermon flies " is the humbling reminder of George Herbert. This man wove a plot. He pictured a moment of desperate need. He brought men to some grave impasse. With deft craftsmanship, he made Religion appear as the only key to the locked door of experience. He was no pietist. He abhorred insincerity, as his unforgettable portrait of Tam Trumbull reveals. Yet he was not unduly severe on the errors of mankind. He had an extraordinary knowledge of human nature. This was amassed in his days at the Scottish bar, and on the bench. He had a worshipful sense.

Even as he wrote, the echoes of old Peter Mathieson's evening Psalter lingered in his ears. He did not require to enter a pulpit. As he pictured life's pilgrimage, it seemed inevitable to his readers that " the way of man is not in himself."

Now, we may wish to have the case established further in a more minute scrutiny of the works. The Introduction to this book has sketched the Method of the Craftsman, and his unconscious spiritual art. What of the content of his message, and the garb in which he clothes it? His appeal to the idyllic is an element that cannot be ignored. To-day in certain Theological schools there is a tendency to belittle the humanities, or to seek to de-spiritualise them. The effect is to produce a hapless dualism. Scott guarded against the danger. He found in all forms of art a revelation divine. From his earliest days he was a lover of Ballad poetry. Something of the rapt intensity of his study of the poets gives urgency and imaginative fire to his religious teaching. In one of the Prefaces to *Scottish Minstrelsy*, he recounts his hours in the Kelso garden as a boy. *Percy's Reliques* in hand, seated on one of the old trees, he imbued the spirit of fancy. The old shepherd at Smailholm Tower, who told his tales in Walter's childhood, had stirred it long before. There was no needless mental divorce in his thinking.

We have been reminded by historians that Homer imbued the legends of every hill, river, and town in ancient Greece. The memory of this made Andrew Lang exclaim of Scott, " Ballads enough the child already knew. Thus he was cradled in Romance, unexampled in the history of modern poets." Professor Herford of Manchester has this illuminating reference to Scott in his *Age of Wordsworth* : " Blending in an unexampled degree the instincts of the poet and the antiquary, he absorbed during his early manhood all the floating treasure of Scottish legend and song. He mastered so far as was then possible the mass of historic and customary lore involved in it. The collector of the Border Minstrelsy was unconsciously becoming the creator of the novels. The romances gathered in these tours came to him with an aroma of open air, a background of heath and glen, which in his hands they never lost."

The mystery of religion and the sense of the sublime in the domain of English Letters were always wedded. There are on the shelves of Abbotsford six volumes in his own handwriting of Scottish poetry. These were collected and copied by him when a student at Edinburgh University. They helped to make more appealing to him Ann Rutherford's Bible in which he penned his affectionate tribute.

He was a reader of the finest lore in French literature. He was a personal friend of Landseer and David Wilkie. It is natural that when he wrote of the Christian faith, something of the spirit hovered about him. He has done for the Creed what Malory did for the Arthurian Knights. We recall that chapter in *Otto* on the *Numenous* in English poetry. It would have appealed to our author, much as did his friendship with little Marjorie Fleming. When he faced the ineffable, or touched the hand of a little child, it was as if God spoke.

PART II

CHAPTER XI

KENILWORTH——IN WARWICKSHIRE AND BY CUMNOR

WE can remember at Oxford standing in the chancel of St. Mary's. There are few more impressive memorials than the tablet so reverently inscribed in memory of Amy Robsart. It is fitting that she should be remembered here. For, if our theory of the influence of the place and environment be reasonable, then Oxford is the shrine where we may linger in her honour. The traditions of the city have most naturally links with the period of Queen Elizabeth. Learning flourished there in her reign with a splendour which is not readily questioned. *Kenilworth* was not published till 1821. Memories of its surroundings must therefore have surged in upon Scott's mind when he wrote. He had visited it for the first time in 1803. That the setting of that seat of learning, its river, and fair countryside, made an impression on him is not a matter of theory. He refers to it once and again in his letters. In one epistle to Miss Seward, he writes of his time there. " It was too short," he says, " to convey to me separate and distinct ideas of all the variety of wonders which I saw." He refers to the pictures in his mind of towers, chapels, oriels and vaulted halls, libraries and paintings. He

87

told another friend that he would have been enchanted to have spent a couple of months among the curious libraries. Cumnor is only a few miles from Oxford. Mr. Buchan in his Life of Scott not only admits the acquaintance of the novelist with Elizabethan lore, but he also fully endorses the spell that Cumnor casts on the narrative in *Kenilworth*. May not something of that love of contrast, so characteristic of all true artists, make more alluring this painter's description of the little village with its old manor house and inn ? If Amy's resting place is under the shadow of that hallowed place where light and learning flourished, then the more secluded and lonely seem the shadowed haunts of that old house where her imprisonment marred her beauty and youth. Travel in the century when Scott lived was more leisurely. It afforded the visitor also greater opportunities of survey in his more reflective passage over the level areas of the district. When Scott describes Cumnor, it is with the skilful hand of realism. There is a sure and graphic touch in his painting. Every unprejudiced reader will admit that Varney, Foster, Janet and their gentle victim play their part the more naturally in the book, because the surroundings are so skilfully weaved into the plot.

Accurate historians admit that the chronology is faulty. The picturesque setting carries the reader on, in forgetfulness of a historical flaw here and there. We are in touch with reality. Above all, human nature is displayed and analysed to us with a masterly touch. We see love and laughter, terror and intrigue, malice and shielding care, patient virtue and unbridled villainy. How could these themes impress us so well if there were not an alliance between the place and the actor ? How could the Drama move with the natural grace that it does, if the whole sequence had not gained something from the light and colour of the scenes that are described ?

Even more this is the case when we view the Castle of Kenilworth, and walk the leafy lanes of Warwickshire. We can never forget our sight of that old stronghold. It is true that at the period of which Scott writes, this lordly seat was not in the hands of the Earl of Leicester. The majesty of the treatment is not affected by the imaginative licence of the novelist. A visit to the Castle in its ruins makes the tale more arresting. Shakespeare when a boy sometimes lingered at the spot where the story of Leicester and Elizabeth is rehearsed. Much of the vividness of the pageantry of the Court life, the revels, the gay music, the regal pomp seems the more full of marvel because Shakespeare in early youth was a witness from afar. So Shakespearean a writer as Scott may have gleaned some of the glamour from the history of the brilliant period with which he was so familiar. He writes as if Shakespeare were already acknowledged a poet. We forgive him for that anachronism. For he breathes the spirit and the charm which the great Elizabethan caught at Kenilworth. It becomes for every reader, as it does for each admiring visitor, a place of haunting memories, built in the masonry of a tangible yet marvellous structure.

The " Mervyn Tower " contains Amy Robsart's room. This is what is called the Strong Tower, which John of Gaunt built. It was only in 1562 that Elizabeth conferred the Castle on Leicester. The garden was on the north side of the Keep. To the west were the Pleasaunce and the Swan Tower, near which Amy was discovered by the Queen. Mr. Findlay Muirhead gives the clue to the universal fame of this old ruin—Sir Walter Scott's romance. The reader carries away a vivid sense of the splendour of the life within its walls. If he can find time to see it, then he will gladly endorse the enthusiast's high estimate of the novelist's rich knowledge of its history, its place in the community's everyday experience, and the sway exercised by Leicester as its lawful lord. Its stately walls, its commanding position, the marks on its ancient walls of the richness of its architecture leave the wayfarer spellbound. Again he appears to enter into the feelings of the displaced Countess, as, footsore and disconsolate, she makes her way thither as a suppliant. It is not difficult to envisage the figure of the Queen, nor to taste the luxurious order of her pleasures. Leicester looks down upon us with his fear-stricken eyes. Tressilian enters sympathetically into the feelings of his deluded friend. Wayland Smith walks the grounds with the daring evasiveness of the merry-maker who is bearing concealed the weight of a deep anxiety for a maiden wronged and rejected. Thus the tragedy of the tale is set over against the background of a local environment. It is partly this that makes the interest of travel to the actual scenes so enthralling. It seems easier to picture the treachery of Varney in such secluded haunts as Cumnor, and to enter into the mental dilemma of Leicester when we have visited Kenilworth. It was the Earl

who said of ' this sworn man, and close brother '
that ' he knew no virtuous property save affection
to his patron.' When Amy looked at him with
contempt in the old manor house, he began his
nefarious work of stifling her power over the Earl.
The death to which he led her was really brought
about by playing with her best affections. The
sound of the horse's hoofs on the avenue seemed so
like the tread of her beloved's steed that she was deceived, and ran to her doom. Lambourne thought
that Foster, who was an instrument in Varney's
undertakings, had been struck out of the book of
life. He imagined him as tormented with the
constant wish to be restored to it. He seems at
home in Cumnor Place. He has leisure there to
frame his schemes, and to reconcile his wavering
mind to principles diverse from his former creed.
No wonder that he was looked on as papist and
puritan, or that Tony Fire the Faggot was the title
which clung to him. No one can forget Janet,
her devotion to her mistress, her quaint unworldly
ways, her far-seeing plans for Amy's escape. The
old house near Oxford was a place of continual
terror for the poor Countess. The one bright spot
was the love and ministry of Janet.

The story of Wayland Smith's visit to the
victim at Cumnor Place as a pedlar is told with
naive and skilful artfulness. The episode of intrigue is penned by Scott as if he had caught the
very atmosphere of these haunts, and the lively
contact of the moving figures in the dialogue. We
feel as we read that something is impending. This
is no mere pedlar's visit. Here is a man, as
Scott describes him, with shrewdness, alertness of

understanding and variety of resource. In the house, he has an open eye for each trivial circumstance, and a ready ear for every casual hint that may be passed to give light upon Amy's situation of peril. Tressilian is behind the scheme. The friction between Sussex and Leicester which appears throughout the book acts as a foil in the contest. It is partly the loyalty of Tressilian to his chief, and partly his own rejected love of Amy that are the channels by which she wins the brief freedom that is hers. The magic of the scene as we look on it at Cumnor Place is that the task of the pedlar is the veil to conceal his serious purpose. Yet who could suspect that such issues hang upon his gay moments as a vendor ?

> " Lawn as white as driven snow,
>   Cyprus black as e'er was crow,
>   Gloves as sweet as damask roses,
>   Masks for faces and for noses."

Wayland Smith is able, too, to warn the prisoner of the ways of Alesco. He is her friend and guide along her fevered way to the Castle. If we have tramped some of the roads that led her there, and if we have seen the curious old city of Warwick, which they passed en route, we will enter vividly into the whole drama, and share its spirit. The novelist knew the spell which such places cast on the traveller. He described Warwick as " the fairest monument of ancient splendour which yet remains uninjured by time." " He has been to Warwick Castle fifty times, if he has been there once," says Charles Dickens in *Dombey and Son*. Not far off stands Stratford-on-Avon. It is an added impulse to enter into the temper of the plot when we are in company with the Elizabethan poet. Did he not as a boy of eleven see the Queen there in 1575? For those who wish to cultivate the mood of sympathetic insight, there are two books of perennial interest. George Morley has written on *Shakespeare's Greenwood*. It is a description of the language, superstitions, customs, folk-lore, birds, etc., of Warwickshire. Archdeacon Hutton has made all travellers his debtors by his scholarly compendium, *Highways and Byways in Shakespeare's Country*. Mr. Edmund New has fascinating illustrations. He has gone over the countryside before his collaborator's impressions were set down. Hutton says that despite the magnificence of the Castle, it might well have been forgotten had it not been for the Wizard of the North. Readers who wish detailed information as to the place are referred to the work of this scholar. Messrs. Macmillan have appended to the book an excellent map. Hutton shows us that it was one of the largest castles of the Norman period. He tells of the architecture, the Tudor windows, the Privy Chamber, Henry VIII's lodgings, Dudley's lobby, the triple defences of the Middle Ages, and the tilt-yard. The ruins of the Castle he regards as the most extensive of any in England. Scott referred to it as " that lordly palace where princes feasted and fought, now in the bloody earnest of storm and siege, and now in the games of chivalry, where beauty dealt the prize which valour won." In the manuscript of Pepys' Diary in Magdalene College, Cambridge, there are particulars as to the visit of the Queen in 1575. It is a fine thought of the Archdeacon's that with these fair surroundings the phantasies and pageant of the place may be woven Shakespeare's description. Oberon sees "Flying between the cold moon and the earth, Cupid all arm'd."

On Scott the picturesqueness of the scenes made a profound impression. Who shall say that place and figures are not linked in immortal fame in the hour where Elizabeth discovers Amy in the Pleasaunce Garden? We know that Laneham's survey of the grounds was of great service to the novelist. He actually visited Kenilworth. In 1815 he stayed in the King's Arms. He writes of his visit many years afterwards. "The relentless rain only allowed us a glimpse of this memorable ruin." Yet he lingered on the spot, and remembered it in minute detail. It is admitted by those who know Kenilworth that still Scott must be our guide if we would go there.

When we stand with him in the Pleasaunce, even in its now inglorious appearance, the setting helps us to understand. We see the pensive figure of Amy. We watch the vigilant look of the Queen. We hear that pathetic tale of the defenceless woman, and we discern the blazing wrath of the bewildered monarch. The quick summons to Dudley, the shame that falls on him before the giddy court, the blight on these days of merry-making, the folly of a deceitful, double life—all are unveiled to us as, with the swift work of a surgeon's instruments, some disease is traced to its hidden source. Kenilworth stands out illumined in the light of conscience. Place and actors become commingled in a picture of rare skill and analytic power.

Kenilworth and Warwickshire

Alas ! how ill-timed the commission to empower Varney to take Amy to Cumnor Place again. Who can but follow breathlessly Leicester's rapid remorse, and his fruitless attempt to stop the flight of his sworn man and close brother ? Again this contrasted portraiture of Scott amazes the reader by its genius. He comes back with Amy dejected from the revels of Kenilworth to the loneliness of Cumnor Place. Never does it seem more forsaken. No hour in the past appears more fateful than that swift moment that plunges her into disaster. We are here in the hands of an artist who has verily imbued the haunting mystery of an unique environment. He has the power to lift us to these scenes in imagination, and yet somehow the splendour and the shadow cannot be explained in terms of earthly language. Here Scott is possessed of that touch of Wordsworth in his genius who brings to the sense of a " light that never was on sea or land."

CHAPTER XII

REDGAUNTLET

THIS tale has its leading centre in the countryside that lies between the mouth of the Annan and that of the Nith. It takes us also over the border into England; and it makes very attractive to the reader the old town of Dumfries. The local colouring is at once seen in the Edinburgh incidents. Scott is writing of the Eighteenth Century in Scotland. When he describes the Scottish capital, he is thinking implicitly of his old home-surroundings. Critics, e.g., such as W. S. Crockett, justly find in Saunders Fairford a picture of the novelist's own father. It is an enchanting thing for the visitor to Edinburgh to view it with the eyes of Scott, as he went to school and to college. He enters into the tumult of boys' frolics at the High School. He crosses the Cowgate-Port. He gains glimpses of the brink of the Castle-rock—the Kittle nine-steps. It was a favourite resort of " the hell and neck boys " of the higher classes. The reader passes in imagination into the old quadrangle of Edinburgh University, and enters the Scotch Law class-rooms. He crosses into the College of Justice, and feels in fancy the black gown of the advocate upon his shoulders. Edinburgh becomes very real when, in the somewhat severe reprimand of Fairford to Alan, we seem to hear an echo of a warning to the romantic Walter in his youth : " You think yourself a wit. . . . ' Unstable as water, he shall not excel,' or as the Septuagint hath it, *Effusa est sicut aqua non crescat.*" Is there not a suggestion of the novelist's own student days in the city, as Alan murmurs : " Latimer, I will tell no lies. I wish my father would allow me a little more exercise of my free-will, were it but that I might feel the pleasure of doing what might please him of my own accord ! " In one of his letters to his friend, Darsie tells him of Dumfries. Later in the tale, this town appears again as the home of Provost Crosbie. The reader has a better idea of the story by lingering in that romantic capital of this southern Scottish country. Darsie tells Alan that Dumfries is built on the gallant river Nith. He reminds him of the tale of Bruce, and his poniard in the Church of the Dominicans, the site of which may still be seen by the traveller. He did not however linger in this old town. He crept along the coast eastwards. He turned towards the Solway Firth. It is this stretch of water that divides the two kingdoms. He looked over to England. Its shores are gilded by the sun's last rays. We found that one of the most convenient ways in which to gain our sense of perspective as we pondered *Redgauntlet* was to cycle from Annan to Caerlaverock Castle and back. The advantage of this is that it gives the reader of the book the picturesque surroundings on which Darsie Latimer's eyes feasted on his tour. We have always to recall the counsel that was given him on his somewhat daring expedition by the rider whom he encountered : " Best make haste, then. He that dreams on the bed of the Solway may wake in the next world.

The sky threatens a blast that will bring in the waves, three feet abreast." It is a treacherous coast, and and the traveller must not dally on the way. Alan in his reply has a vivid touch. He had been thinking in Edinburgh of the tempest that had overtaken his friend. Evidently it had been no local happening : " As for the affair of Thursday last, it roared, whistled, howled and bellowed, as fearfully among the old chimney-heads in the Candlemaker Row as it could on the Solway shore, for the very wind of it—*teste me per totam noctem vigilante*." He urges Darsie not to allow his love of adventure too far. He aptly repeats a phrase in *Lear*, as he shows that the storm might have proved " a naughty night to swim in." Yet from the point of view of the reader of Scott who is committed to the view that these Essays seek to prove, it is the ardour of Darsie's adventures which lend the colour and the enterprise to *Redgauntlet* of which romantic people can never tire.

It is generally surmised that Mount Sharon, where Latimer for a while found his home (although it is presented to us in the region we have described), is a reminiscence of Henrysyde. When Scott was a little lad in Kelso School, his lameness sometimes kept him from play. He had permission from the owners of Henrysyde to find a literary haunt here. This lovely home helped to form in him the taste for reading. This is confirmed by Sir Walter. He speaks of his few acquaintances in these Kelso days, and of the scarcity of books. In this Quaker's home he was allowed to roam at pleasure, and to turn to its well-stored shelves. We remember being permitted to spend a lovely

afternoon there by its verdant lawns, its well-stored
library, and its much-prized paintings. The windows look out over the meadows to the river. It
is easy to picture Walter amidst these surroundings.
With the memory of that home in his mind, Mount
Sharon was the more readily pictured. The weaving
of such a recollection as was his into the texture
of his narrative is a fresh instance of his power
as an artist, and of the link between his own personal
travels and the places in his books. Scott describes
it as " an Eden of beauty, comfort, and peace."
Joshua Geddes who lived there was a Quaker, too,
a partner in the Tide-net Fishing Company. He
was a man of indomitable courage, who had caught
something of the high impulse of his rich surroundings. Neither the floods of water, nor the
fear of the snare, nor the drawn sword of the
adversary could frustrate his designs. Scott dwells
on the beauty of the situation, its pleasure-ground,
its honeysuckle and clematis, as if memory had
indeed been stirred as he penned his lines. His
descriptions, too, include the interior, and he revives
his readers' recollections of a paper in *The Spectator*
where some such alliance of outward loveliness
with inward beauty is unveiled.

Much as the more cultivated grace of Mount
Sharon was enjoyed, there is that in the open life
of the Southern lands of Scotland that enchanted
Darsie as much as did the charms of Henrysyde
the youthful Walter. Perhaps there was the more
enjoyment in his unrestricted liberty, as he remembered the more circumscribed life of the city.
We cannot fail to trace again an autobiographical
touch in Saunders Fairford's reference to his son

in his letter to the Solway wanderer. He writes of how apt he has been to keep Alan from his studies. The student of law in the Eighteenth Century appears to share the professional limitations of the novelist in his Edinburgh days. For the father writes : " Alan has the world to win ; and louping and laughing as you and he were wont to do, would soon make the powder flee out of his wig, and the pence out of his pocket." There are recurrent notes in these personal allusions that make the father of Sir Walter and Saunders Fairford companion pictures. In the sight of the shining Firth, in the free air, in the clouds with their varied tints, Darsie finely compares himself to Bunyan's Pilgrim who on his liberated way broke forth into song.

We may seek in vain on the banks of the Solway to discover the locus of certain descriptions of *Redgauntlet*. We cannot fail at least to feel the spirit of these haunts which unmistakably mirror the imagery of the book. There is a curious sense of mystery in the quiet nooks and leisurely scenes of that district, its knolls and sand-pits, its secluded villages and dreamy guises that convince us that Scott knew that land and water well.

Indeed, on the gravestone of a little churchyard we saw an inscription which brought us very near the music which so often was warbled by hill and dale. It is the memorial to one whose figure, some think, is enshrined as Wandering Willie in the plot. When his faithful wife described him, this is her unforgettable record of him : " Ye ken mickle less of my hinnie, sir, that thinks he needs ony guiding; he's the best guide himsel' that ye'll find between

Criffel and Carlisle. Horse-road and foot-path, parish road and kirk-road, high-road and cross-road, he kens ilka foot of good ground round Nithsdale."

This is the director along these difficult roads whose identity some connect with the blind fiddler whose resting-place is in the Kirkyard of Twynholm. So impressed were the clergy of the neighbourhood with this man's gifts and his endurance in face of difficulties, that they raised this memorial. Mr. Dick in his *Byways of Galloway* tells of his battles in Egypt, of the loss of his sight and of his return to Scotland as a minstrel. When he married, and children grew up about him, it was hard to find support. Together the family wandered in Galloway. One bitter night they sought in vain for shelter. Hospitality was persistently refused them. In desperation, they lay down to rest in some earthen hollow. They imagined that they were protected by the overhanging ground. In the night, when they were asleep, the crag above them gave way with the force of the tempest. They were submerged. The only survivor was the donkey that carried the little children, one by one, along the roads that the fiddler knew so well, but whose sun-lit beauty it was left to Scott to disclose. Whether this quaint heroic minstrel be the original of Willie Steenson, it is not possible to say conclusively. There is sufficient resemblance to make it not unnatural to conjecture he may have been.

At all events, Rockhall in Dumfriesshire is the spot where there is for ever enshrined the memory of Wandering Willie's Isle. In the world's literature there are few short stories to rival it.

Scott and the Lure of the Road

Rockhall was the home of Sir Robert Grierson of Lag, the henchman of Claverhouse, who made it his unceasing task, in the Killing times, to bring to strict examination, and if needs be, to death, the enemies of the cause of the King. It is a property rich in interest to every lover of history and of Scott. Some readers, by turning to it in thought, may be the more readily enticed to hear the strains of Wandering Willie's minstrelsy and to read his immortal tale. In Darsie's servitude in Cumberland, he ended his song as Cristal Nixon approached with the lines :

> " Leave thee—leave thee, lad—
> I'll never leave thee ;
> The stars shall gae withershins,
> Ere I will leave thee."

The Scottish Community Association staged one scene from the episode in *Redgauntlet*. This is the visit of Willie and Darsie to the fishermen's dance at Broken Burn. At Rockhall we are shown the place where Grierson's horses were stabled. The saddles were on the horses' backs all night, ready to be mounted, the stable light always burning that Lag and his emissaries might ride out in search of their prey. The neighbouring railway-station is somewhat ominously called *Rack*—a pathetic reminder of the sufferings of the victims of Redgauntlet's fury. In the dungeon there is exhibited the iron hook on which the prisoners were strung in the hour of execution. " Glen nor dargle nor mountain nor cave could hide the puir hill-folk when Redgauntlet was out with bugle and blood-hound after them. Troth when they found them, they didna' mak

muckle mair ceremony than a Hielandman wi'
a roebuck—it was just, " Will ye tak' the test ?
If not, Make-ready—Present—Fire, and there lay
the recusant."

The great oak parlour is evidently the work of
Scott's imagination. Rockhall does not boast of
such a room as described. Steenie seems to
follow us as we move about the old mansion, and we
can almost hear the sough of his pipes. The "ill-
favoured jackanape " must have given the minstrel
a weird sense of lonesomeness. It was not easy to
remain complacent in the presence of Redgauntlet—
his broadsword and his pistols were too close at hand !
We climb the stairway, and then we view the old
stone steps up which the jackanape went with the
silver whistle. We seem to hear it again among the
chimneys, turrets and bartizans. When we read of
the loss of the whistle, there seems a strange and
uncanny sense of mystery. We heard a practical
person who knew well the history of the Grierson
family say, " The loss of the whistle is easily
explained. It was the funeral day and everyone
was drunk."

In Rockhall the awesome gathering of stern
soldiers of history appears very real—Middleton,
Lauderdale, Rothes and the rest. If we have made
our way to Dumfries by Castle-Douglas, the scene is
the more realistic. For, are not the words quoted
of the bloody Earl of Douglas at Threeve Castle ?—
" It's ill speaking between a fou' man and a
fasting " ? The sound of this stinging question
startles us as we leave the ancient halls—" Weel,
piper, hae ye settled wi my son for the year's
rent ? " In his better moments, at least, the true

Scot has a deep reverence for the leading of the Church. It is not incredible that Steenie after his unspeakable experiences of terror in Rockhall should resolve to delate himself to the Presbytery. He proposes to tell them all he has seen, " whilk," he adds, " are fitter for them to judge of than a borrel like me."

There are other roads that open for us as we tread our path with Darsie. None is quite so memorable as that which leads us to this scene of the doings of that night when Redgauntlet was called to his account. It is not our present task to suggest any psychological analysis. If it were, we should have been inclined to enlarge on the ethical phases of a soul summoned to judgment, the place of Nemesis, and the power that Scott has as a novelist to disclose the more serious issues of life.

It may almost be a relief to the reader to find himself in Parliament House, and to feel the wittier aspect of Peter Peebles's fifteen years' legal pleas. Here again, local colour is explained by Scott's early life as an advocate. None but one deeply stored in the technicalities of the Court of Session could have painted so well the doings of these judicial courts. " It is grandeur upon earth," says Peter, " to hear ane's name thundered out along the long-arched roof of the outer House. Poor Peter Peebles against Plainstaves, *et per contra* ; a' the best lawyers in the house fleeing like eagles to the prey ; some because they are in the cause, and some because they want to be thought engaged. To see a' this, and to ken that naethin' will be said or done amang a' thae folk for maybe the feck of three hours, saving what concerns you and your business——

O man, nae wonder that ye judge this to be earthly glory."

Annan, where Tom Trumbull, "the grizzled hypocrite," dwelt, is mentioned more than once in *Redgauntlet*. The traveller will find the conditions very much as the novelist describes them, except that to-day the citizen lives by more honest means of sustenance. The trade in which Tom earned his livelihood is no mere fiction. Scott adds a note to his novel to describe one similar rendezvous of smugglers in Spittal, Berwick, with secret communication in the roof, and trap-door. Trumbull was the associate of outlaws and of smugglers.

In the days about which Scott wrote this tale it was a common thing to cross over the Solway to England. We have little difficulty, as we stand on the banks of the estuary, in picturing Nanty Ewart, of the Jumping Jenny, bringing Prince Charlie from Dunkirk, or escorting Alan to Cumberland. Certainly a visit to the town of Annan makes more enthralling the scene that Scott draws. When we recall that here Edward Irving ministered and Carlyle acted as a schoolmaster, we are brought to the remembrance of a trinity of names that are treasured in the archives of learning. So wide was Scott's knowledge of these Islands of ours that his descriptions are culled sometimes from districts far apart from the locus of his novel. It is a rare pleasure for the traveller, passing southward from Edinburgh to break his journey on the high road to Moffat at the Devil's Beef-tub, to slide down the grassy slope by the roadway to that hiding-place, to imagine a day of mist, and to conjure anew the doings of the soldiers' march which Scott has so well described with the deft escape to that place of shelter. " It is the way of our house," says Redgauntlet, " our courage ever rises highest on the losing side." Not alone on the Moffat road, but in the whole moving drama of *Redgauntlet* is this saying of the hero made good.

A scene where the setting seems to be finely wed to the light and the music which Scott allows to play on the figures, is in Crakenthorp's inn in Cumberland. " Never a warrant he hears of it afore the ink's dry." This is the meeting-place of the long-separated friends, Allan Fairford and Darsie Latimer. As Darsie passed the blind fiddler he asked could he not play a Scottish air ? The dull mechanism of Willie's previous melody is changed to a flood of inspiration. Friendship stirs the heart to music. It is not only the fiddler that is inspired. Scott surely shows his powers as an artist when the chords of communication are opened between Darsie and Wandering Willie. If we are led to follow his melody, we are also prompted to travel with him the path that he has made so enticing. In *As You Like It*, from which Scott has gleaned his motto, we hear the harmonious call of that shining road :

> " Master go on : and I will follow thee,
>   To the last gasp, with truth and loyalty."

CHAPTER XIII

THE FAIR MAID OF PERTH

A PHASE of our author's genius is the selective power that he showed in his choice of the ground for each novel. This power of choice is nowhere more marked than in this tale. It is a story of the era of Robert the Third. By what gift of insight does he find the setting for a mediæval outlook and custom so fitting as that of this old town lying at the centre of Scotland ? There is everything here to give the Drama its free movement. The sheltering hills are Nature's defence. The broad-flowing Tay provides the channel of ready transit. The ancient city, with its traditions, its buildings, its broad Inch (as it prepared for the conflict of the clans) all are part of the texture of the story. The majesty of the setting is not only at one with the atmosphere that the novelist creates. It is also the witness to his discerning eye. That he should have the æsthetic sense to discover it is a literary dowry which perhaps appreciative writers are not too lavish to admit.

Scott was enamoured of the whole district, and he poetically writes of " beauty lying in the lap of terror." The antiquity of Perth also appealed to him. It was the home of kings. They had no continuous palace there, but they found shelter in the convent. He describes with rapture the valley of the Tay, the meadows, steeples and towers of the town, the hills of Kinnoull and Moncrieff with the Grampians in the distance. It all becomes a fitting stage for late fourteenth-century history, and for the ascent to the throne of Robert the Third. To-day we may visit the old church of St. John, which the liberality of the late Lord Forteviot has brought to its pristine beauty. We seem to have caught the worshipful spirit of the old Dominican church. Simon Glover entered it when oppressed by care. " He knelt down," says Scott, " with the air of a man who has something burdensome on his mind, but when the service was ended, he seemed free from anxiety, as of one who had referred himself and his troubles to the disposal of Heaven." The High Church of St. John is again presented to the reader's view after the murder scene. The prominence given to it (as anyone who visits it may readily realise) was prompted by the good taste of the admirer of its structure. The Protestant revolt against outward beauty is somewhat pathetically instanced by the later historians of the Reformation. St. John's was the Church fixed on for the furious action of " the rabble multitude " in the days of John Knox. The citizens owning the Roman faith were justly proud of it. It was " their ain good auld St. John." The eastern window in its rich and varied tints, the high altar, impressed all who viewed them. We can recall standing with Lord Forteviot in the nave after its restoration, and we cannot but rejoice that that worshipful sense which the view of the chancel makes possible is the privilege anew in the Church of St. John of all lovers of our common faith.

The Fair Maid of Perth

It is evident that the sense of the loveliness of the church and its surroundings was well noted by the Glover family. The Fair Maid's reputed house may still be seen. But it may be that the interest of the reader of the tale will be deepened, as he shares something of her love for the less restricted surroundings of the broad, open countryside. At that period, this fringed her dwelling not far from the river-side. There is an enthusiasm in her mind for that regal worth of Nature on which Sir Walter's eye also feasted with delight. Catherine is speaking —" I promise you, father, that when I crossed the Wicks of Baiglie and saw the bonny city lie stretched before me like a queen of romance, whom the Knight finds asleep among the wilderness of flowers, I felt even as a bird, when it folds its wearied wings to stoop down on its own nest."

The narrow alleys and streets of the town have still about them the old-world air of these distant days. As we walk through the older parts we seem to hear the echo of the Ballad :

> " Within the bonds of Annandale,
>   The gentle Johnstones ride ;
>   They have been there a thousand years,
>   A thousand more they'll bide."

The East-end of the High Street is suggested as the Port at which the deputation from Kinfauns met. The bridge was a lordly structure across which the councillors passed. It is described *Sancti Joannis pontem ingentem apud Perth*. It seems to have been repaired by Robert the Bruce. King Robert the Third had something of the vacillation of Richard the Second. He lacked the warlike qualities appropriate to the times. His son, the Duke of Rothesay was giddy and feeble. Perth and the country generally was disturbed by his revels. If not for the good of his nephew, at least for his own ends, the Duke of Albany encourages a greater restraint of Rothesay. He is all for a more effectual corrective. The doings of the glee-woman, the feckless character of the Prince, the rivalry of Douglas and Albany, the hesitation of the King to act with determined force are happily in keeping with the background of the ancient city of Perth. There is the temper, too, of the true antiquarian in the introduction of Simon and his timely craft. These artisans were of high standing, and they date back to a very early period. One of the shrines in old St. John's had charters connected with their order. A banner of theirs, dating from 1604, has these words inscribed on it, " The perfect honour of a craft or beauty of a trade is not in wealthe, but in moral worth whereby virtue gains renown."

Scott, too, with all his antique studies, manages to relate his characters appositely to men and women whom he himself has known. In his biography, it is interesting to find that Conacher, who was taken into the employment of Simon the Glover in the tale, is treated with an added charity, despite his timidity because of the author's own unhappy experience with Daniel, his own brother. Conacher was a man of honour, but in some respects his weaknesses resemble those of Scott's brother. Sir Walter in earlier days had treated this relative with some coldness and lack of forbearance. In later life he had greatly repented of his aloofness from Daniel. Lockhart shows that the generous estimate which

Scott gives of Conacher's character is a reflex of Scott's own family life. This is another instance of the fact that the light and shade, the by-play and dramatic interest of these stories of Scott's are not entirely the fruit of detached literary enterprise. They are the evidence, as Mr. Buchan has shown us so conclusively in his Centenary Speech at Selkirk, that in mingling with the throng, in entering into intimate links of affection with his fellows, Scott has become the true delineator of mankind. It is perhaps little wonder that those who visited Lord Rosebery in the last decade of his life found that rare bookman lingering so often over one or other of the volumes of the Wizard of the North.

Could the reader of the Waverley novels suggest any other part of Scotland which could have so well formed the historic centre for the tragic doings of King Robert's reign ? Is not this the natural playground for the Prince's frolics ? Does not the old town of Perth, with its meal-vennel, wynds and High Street, seem the fitting centre for raids, for love scenes and assaults, for nocturnal revels and murders ? May we not imagine the Earl of March riding down its roads, as he fixed his envious eye on Douglas ? Does not the North Inch stand out in Scott's treatment as the living battlefield of unbridled forces ? Could his delineation of the Convent, and the Fathers of the Church, be excelled ? Curfew Street, where Catherine lived, becomes real to us, and we follow the revellers after Oliver's feat with the feeling that we are indeed in their terrifying presence. So lit with realism is the description of the book. We stand in the presence of the Prince. "Let us help him now, my Lord," says Ramorny to him. "I am possessed of a dreadful secret. Albany hath been trafficking with me to join him in taking your Grace's life." Then the Master of the House goes on to describe to him his plot on the life of the Duke of Albany and the dethroning of his father. To those who have visited the east coast of Fifeshire, it gives a fresh touch of vividness to find the villainous Ramorny on the rejection of his scheme claiming to desire to exchange lance and saddle for the breviary and the confessional. With a pitiable insincerity he pictures himself a meditative inmate of Lindores Abbey, with quiet to ponder the psalm.

It is in graphic touches such as this that Scott lifts the reader to regions familiar to him in the countryside which he knew so well. Skilfully does he bring the reader back to the surroundings nearest to him. Lindores, with its peaceful abbey, is not at this period the resting-place of either. The Prince is taken to Constable's lodgings, the residence of the Earl of Erroll. No one who has read the dialogue that took place there can readily forget the tragical setting, the condemning charge of Albany, the surprise of the Prince at the deadly treatment meted out to Bonthron the dark satellite. The lodgings were at the end of the Water-gate. In this part of the town most of the nobility were resident. There were gardens which went as far as the city walls, close to the Tay. Scott pictures the Prince's desolation in these quarters. He asked for the presence of Sir John Ramorny. The pavilion in the High Constable's garden becomes in the novelist's hands the scene of intrigue and revenge. Ramorny is only too glad to meet one who has done him so many ills. " It was only for your Royal Highness's personal freedom," says this subtle adviser, " that I was presuming to speak. Were I in your Grace's place, I would get me into that good boat which hovers on the Tay and drop quietly down to Fife where you have many friends, and make free use to take possession of Falkland. It is a royal castle, and though the King has bestowed it in gift on your uncle, yet surely even if the grant were not subject to challenge, your Grace might make free with the residence of so near a relative." The insinuating plea that Ramorny and Dwining make to the Prince has the witchery of the most evil form of all temptation. It is the work of a rare artist in words to portray, as the novelist does, the departure from the Constable's lodgings. Place and setting are lit by that local colour which this narrator knew so well how to shed on his canvas. He paints the moving ebb-tide, the old Castle of Kinfauns within sight, which visitors remember so well, the glee-woman with her bewitching music. The dirge in Norman-French is wafted on the waters of the Tay :

> " Yet thou mayst sigh,
> And look once more at all around,
> At stream, and bank, and sky, and ground,
> Thy life its final course has found,
> And thou must die."

The Prince and his attendants have arrived at Newburgh. At the village, at that time devoted to fishing, there are horses in readiness. Their voyage, as we may readily discover, may be accomplished by boat. From there it is but eight miles to Falkland. We have walked over the ground and caught sight, as we approached, of the tower of the old palace there. Into it he was taken, not in royal splendour, but as a prisoner. Historians, such as Dr. Hume Brown, hesitate to conclude that Rothesay's death was accomplished at the willing instigation of his uncle. How far the episode is true to history as related by Scott we cannot well say. So powerfully has he impressed the popular imagination, that to-day visitors are shown the opening in the dungeon where the grain was passed through the iron grating to keep the prisoner in life. Of this we may be sure, that the Duke of Albany had bitterly resented that he himself should have been displaced from his office of Guardian of Scotland. In the episode that relates to the earlier life of the Duke of Rothesay, the Scottish Community Drama well depicts the hapless sparks of folly that helped to quicken the flame of hatred. This does not excuse Albany. It adds to the pathos of the Prince's fate. On the pages of the book there is an echo of Byron's couplet :

> "Ah me ! in sooth he was a shameless wight,
> Sore given to revel, and ungodly glee."

When Catherine is with the Prince in these tense moments in the palace we cannot help turning to the thought of *Comus*. We remember the fine sense of purity which in the presence of the worst of men Milton shows may be a shield to the defenceless. It is with a sigh of relief that we find ourselves with Catherine Glover outside the room where he lies in misery, the victim of others' cruelty, but worst of all, the bondsman of his own weakness. "Now be present with me, Heaven, she had prayed, and Thou wilt, if I forsake not myself." Who shall say that there is nothing in the *genius loci* of this skilled narrator? If he visit Falkland, the student will be foremost in urging that all that ballad, poetry, history, nature and place can furnish, the craftsman Scott has imbued, and that he has learned his craftsmanship with master-hand. The evil intent of the Prince on the one hand, and on the other her lowly ministry of love, as along with the glee-woman she passes through the grating what will allay the Prince's thirst, such scenes as these demand no comment. The atmosphere is so charged with terror that not even the reader can remain long at Falkland. Then the bells for vesper begin to ring. It is with a feeling of relief that along with Catherine we hear the clatter of the milk-pitchers as the farm woman passes into the kitchen. We are taken from high tragedy to the simplicity of lowly life. To this Scott always bids us return. There is nothing super-mundane or ecstatic in his portraiture of life. The route along which he leads us may sometimes be a stiff ascent, but as we come with him to Perth again we feel that the road to which he leads us is filled with the interests that are ours to-day. This is always the mark of the true artist.

It is little wonder if one of the best of literary critics admits that an author " never wrote a better novel of adventure." He reveals, as other historians do, that it was *on his way to St. Andrews* that the Prince was beset by Albany. We are not the less filled with admiration at the dramatic turn that Scott gives to his tale, transferring grim events to

Scott and the Lure of the Road

Falkland. For the test of a novelist is not his undeviating fidelity to history, but his power to make the enduring things of human joy and tragedy authenticate their own potency on our imaginations and our hearts.

We are continually impressed with the author's detailed interest in contemporary facts that light up his narrative and which justify incidents which had otherwise remained inexplicable. A good example of this is given by Mr. Andrew Lang. He points out that at a particular period, Simon Glover is separated from his daughter in Perth on a charge of heresy. This is no unreal freak of Scott's imagination. Lang points out that in St. Andrews University at that period there were masters of the College, a certain Master Laurence, of Lindores, holding forty heretical views at the very period concerning which *the Fair Maid of Perth* is concerned. Spottiswood mentioned that Laurence was burned at Perth in 1407. The historian here is inaccurate in his records. Laurence died in 1437, and technically could not be regarded as a heretic. That he was charged with false doctrine is at least an evidence that Simon Glover's case was not exceptional. Thus while here and there the pedant may lay the onus on Sir Walter because his tales occasionally lead the reader from the rigid path of accurate detail, Scott may well have this apology, that his mind is steeped in a mass of detail which in other less-observed ways give historicity to his descriptive passages. He seldom errs in his scenic effects, nor is he fanciful in his analysis of human nature. Besides, the road along which his pilgrims travelled gave rise to rapt converse and exciting incident. They live in stirring times. If in these days we are a little more prosaic, is it not something to be coveted that we examine our track over these fair isles of ours more leisurely, and discover in them much of the glamour that he saw? When the glee-woman and Catherine stood on the parapet of the Palace, they had need of some cordial such as this material age has for jaded hearts. "Do the horrors of Falkland still weigh down your spirits?" said Louise. "Strive to forget them as I do: we cannot tread life's path lightly, if we shake not from our mantles the rain-drops as they fall."

CHAPTER XIV

THE BLACK DWARF AND PEEBLESSHIRE

By the Manor Water in Peeblesshire, four miles south-west of Neidpath Castle, stands the Cottage of the Black Dwarf. Since Scott's visit in 1797 it has been rebuilt. It is well worth seeing even in its more modern state, for it calls up memories of a tale which to the reader who digs deep enough in its hidden meaning is a fascinating story. The Dwarf's real name was Ritchie, and his bodily deformities and his somewhat diabolic tendencies made him a centre of interest in the neighbourhood. Even on the anatomical side he drew forth many comments from physiologists. For a considerable time after his death his extraordinary physical structure was preserved in the Surgeons' Hall Museum in Edinburgh. There were many names applied to him. Elshender, the Recluse, Canny Elshie, the Wise man of Mucklestane Moor, the Solitary. In the tale he is referred to as " a mis-shapen monster, with a distorted resemblance to humanity." He professed to have one leading purpose—to add to the mass of misery of his fellow-men. He felt deeply any reference to his infirmity, and because of this he disliked children, who saw in him only a target for their ridicule. In earlier years he had loved a kinswoman. Ellieshaw had been treacherous to the Black Dwarf, and displaced him. Thus he became the victim of suffering. His body was handed over to " chains, his hand to guilt, his soul to misery." He became a misanthropist. Byron somewhere writes of " the bitter blasphemy of the spirit against the unkindness of nature." It is illustrated here. In his seclusion in some ways he resembles Timon of Athens. Yet we shall discover, as we read the doings of Black Dwarf to the end, that there are unsuspected self-sacrifices in his life, and also extraordinary powers of chivalrous and forgiving love. Ritchie had been a native of Stobo, in Tweeddale. He had served for some time as a brush-maker, but he was subjected to so many taunts from his fellow-workmen that he had to end these labours. It was said also that in the night-time he collected the stones to build his simple dwelling in Peeblesshire, and he did it in disregard of the rights of the proprietor on whose land he erected it. To employ the phrase of Falstaff, " *His was a fair house built on another's ground.*" Here again Scott shows his normal fidelity to conditions of place. He pictures the countryside as it actually is. He even writes of the patch of moorland and of the farm of Woodhouse. Readers of Scottish history are familiar with the name of Burnett of Barns. His property lies close by. In fact, in walking to the cottage from Lyne station, it is possible to pass through the grounds of Barns. The tower goes back much earlier than Burnett's time, to 1498. It is known as the Howlet, because of the marauding expeditions at night in olden times. There was a number of such old towers in the district. We have learned of about a dozen of them. When we come to a later stage in the book, we shall find other

Scott and the Lure of the Road

instances of historical and geographical honesty which convince us again that our fiction writer is dealing with the foundations of actual fact as a basis. Apart from this, there is the eye for outer loveliness which reveals the bona-fide wayfarer on the land. It was not a fruitless harvest that rewarded Scott's visit to Hallyards, where he was the guest of his friend, Adam Ferguson. If he had had the rhythmic touch in poetry that he himself admired in Burns, and which he often has in his prose, he might have penned words as melodious as those which a lover of the Borders has enshrined in his *Highways and By-ways*.

> "In its far glens Manor outspreads its arms
> To all the hills, and gathers to itself
> The burnies breaking from high mossy springs,
> And white streaks that fall through clearing of the crags,
> From lonely lochans where the curlews cry."

If there still remain readers unconvinced that our author is not influenced by actual surroundings, let them turn to the drawing of Hugh Thomson. As he sees Peebles from Neidpath, or looks up that stretch of water which poet and artist rival each other to reveal, the pilgrim will be glad that Scott loved these Border lands so well, and that there is the sense and taste of them in *The Black Dwarf*. When we reach the dialogue between Isabel Vere and Elshender in his dismal dwelling, we have an actual production in essence of Scott's own experience when he was in the presence of this strange, uncanny lad. The stay at Hallyards gave him the opportunity of calling on Ritchie. It left an indelible impression on him.

The Black Dwarf and Peeblesshire

The door-way is very low, and men of average height have to stoop to enter. When Scott did so, the Dwarf locked the door from within and he was left to speak with him. With a grasp of iron the Dwarf held his wrist and asked him " Whether he had the po'er?" He meant was he possessed of some magical dynamic? It is said that Scott's face became pale as ashes. The whole demeanour of the man, his abnormal build, his fierce and solitary ways of life, his almost threatening attitude were never forgotten by the visitor. Need we marvel that he is able to convey to us in the story that contact with a creature whose repellent ways after all these years leave us bewildered and surprised?

That Scott should see more desirable traits in him, and that he should weave that sense of trustfulness of the man into his novel, is what we should expect from a personality such as the author's. How many brought into contact with a figure three and a half feet high, shoeless and irritable, able with his skull to strike through the panel of a door, would have been desirous to discover redeeming qualities? Scott showed that this strange being was fond of Shenstone's *Pastorals*, of Allan Ramsay, and was a student of Milton. He made a fair garden from the wild moorland. He spoke of immortality with tears. If there was a more wistful hope in the mind of such a man of a life beyond, was it because of the humbling infirmities of this life? With an intensity difficult for the normal person to realise, would he not fathom hidden meanings in the phrase, " this corruptible shall put on incorruption "?

Scott and the Lure of the Road

We have argued that *fidelity to actual scenes* gives to Scott's romanticism an appeal which makes it sublime. It would be possible to illustrate this lucidly from this novel in more than one detail. We do not know anything in Art which is a better parallel to it than the work of the pre-Raphaelite School. Dante Gabriel Rossetti and some of his compeers last century accomplished in the West of Scotland an enduring labour of loveliness. In one of the works of this group of painters, we have one such actual happening idealised. In the captivity of James the First, Lady Beaufort, as she walked in the garden, stirred the sense of poetry in the royal heart. He wrote of it in lines that still are read. The echoes of such a couplet as this lingered in D. G. Rossetti's memory :

> " And on hir hede a chaplet fresch of hewe,
> Off plumys partit rede and quhite and blewe."

In *The King's Quhair*, scenes such as these are depicted. Rossetti himself ventured to extend the tale in a poem of his own. That actual blend of history and idyllic grace are enshrined in work which may still be seen on the stone walls of a spiral stairway of an old Scottish keep, painted by one of that group. In literature, we have the same kinship on the pages of Scott. Dr. John Brown, in his *Horae Subsecivae*, has shown that the Black Dwarf's love of flowers in his real life by Manor Water is authenticated, and especially the high worth that he set on roses. Readers of the novel will remember that the plot of the tale turns on Isabel Vere's acceptance of the rose that he gave to her.

The Black Dwarf and Peeblesshire

It was the pledge of his championship of her cause. If ever she was in difficulty or in danger, she was to return it to him.   Now it is an admitted fact that there was one species of rose which this strange character in Peeblesshire only gave to three. One old lady was proud in later life to produce the faded leaves of this καλλιστεῖον from the pages of her Bible. It is a faded rose that in the novel Isabel exhibits to the Black Dwarf in her hour of peril. Few things are more moving in the tale than the power this flower and her winning face have to awaken unexpected sacrifice in this misshapen hater of mankind. It is part of the immortal worth of Sir Walter that he leads us to see that even in the worst of men there is some chord that will answer to goodness.   In criticism of the book, it is not always remembered that unconsciously he has made this contribution to ethics by wedding the circumstances of that desolate dwelling by Manor Water to the glorious hour of Isabel's romantic deliverance to which the sequel introduces us.

> " Who sees a rose with loving eyes,
> Though he lack learning is full wise ;
> And he who cares for bird or beast,
> Is of God's servants not the least.
>
> For once the Lord of earth and sky
> Deigned in a humble crib to lie,
> And He who all creation had,
> Looked on the lilies and was glad."

This is not the occasion to examine the nexus of the plot, nor the dramatic development which Scott's treatment lends to it.   There is evidence in the construction of a very close contact with his figures.

Scott and the Lure of the Road

If it be true, as may well be argued, that the deeds
that are portrayed might be acted in any other
County, this is only half a truth. There is inevitably
the atmosphere of that sylvan Border-land. The
men and women who move before us have the accent
and the bearing of these sturdy chiels. Professor
Minto has pointed out that "owing to the bitterness
of Border feuds, reconciliations were antecedently
incredible ; a Border audience would hardly have
believed in them as possible except through supernatural interference, and the agents whom Scott
employs were perfectly familiar to Border superstition." It has been aptly pointed out by one who
had studied the life of the Ettrick shepherd, that the
discussion in the first chapter on " the long sheep "
and " the short sheep " actually stirred Hogg's
suspicions that the writer of the tales was a Borderer.
He asked, " Can this even be Sir Walter ? " In
addition, there is the discontent which these strong
men shared, and there is a marked Jacobite feeling.
Indeed, the political situation is partly responsible
for the vacillation of Isabel's father in the hour of
her peril. It is a truer estimate of the grave moral
weakness of the man to say that he allowed the
national situation to weigh with him as an excuse
for leading her to the altar. To permit her to marry
a man to save his own life in that most threatening
situation was surely a craven part. The point of
value for us in our survey of Scott's constructive
art in *The Black Dwarf* is that, like all wise story-
tellers, he sets the local circumstances in line with
a bigger movement, affecting the whole land.
Hazlitt, in his famous essay on *The Spirit of the Age*,
goes out of his way to protest against Scott's anti-

quarian interest. He calls him " *laudator temporis
acti*," a prophesier of things past. " The old world
is to him a crowded map ; the new one a dull,
hateful blank." Again he complains that " no Red
Reiver of Westburnflat sets fire to peaceful cottages."
The burden of Hazlitt's criticism of Scott in this
particular is that he is detached from the present.
Surely this is an unfair charge against him. Our
plea is that as he recasts history the present becomes
more real. We are the more interested in the
romance and tragedy of Manor Water when we
recall the doings of Prince Charlie. The chapters
in his life have a relation to the scenes in the life of
the devotees. Some of them too were expecting
aid from France in support of his cause. It was the
purpose of more than a few at least to further their
own personal ends by devotion to his crusade.
Scott admits that difficulties in their own lot, or
national resentment, formed part of their motives in
the fray. The light and shade in that picture are
the more artful in that we are led to wider horizons,
and see little things in the truer proportion of a
larger world. The same mingled aims too that
affected the men of Manor Water appear in all grave
issues that touch human nature in its changing
moods. They are found in *Henry the Fourth*, when
Shakespeare, with his mastery of phrase, has this
vivid summary of the struggle :

" To face the garment of rebellion
  With some fine colour that may please the eye."

This kinship with the affairs of the period through
which he makes his pilgrims walk, is one of the
canons of literary worth by which Scott should be

tested. " What choice remains," asks Vere, " between this lot and the ignominious scaffold? Nothing can save me but reconciliation with these men ; and to accomplish this I have promised that Isabel shall marry him 'ere midnight. . . . I have but one remedy betwixt me and ruin."

This inter-relation between local events and the wider struggle of the country is the more worth marking. For it is often unnoticed when comments on the *Black Dwarf* are made, that Scott's sense of perspective comes out in somewhat subtle ways. The cause of Charlie he knows is doomed. The rumoured supporting arms from France never had any real bearing on the contest. That cause, as we shall find more fully in *Waverley*, is lost. The comfort in the story before us is that Isabel's protest wins the day. As the old play has it :

> " 'Twas time and griefs that framed him thus,
>   Time with his fairer hand,
>   Offering the fortunes of his former days,
>   The former man may make him."

Our author is sometimes accused (as our Introduction on his Craftsmanship suggests) of not sufficiently touching the really deep things of life—the mystery and the Cross which are part of the lot of wayfaring man. Can anyone make this charge sincerely after reading the dialogue in this tale between Elliot and his grandmother ? He has lost all that made life worth living. He has been deprived of the bounties that most he prized on earth. There is something in that intense inward struggle of the sorrowful farmer that has touches in it of the *Drama of Job*. It comes too in the simpler guise of a Borderer's grief. Nevertheless, it has links with the same elemental problems, our disappointed ambitions, our baffled dreams of promise. We do not need, of course, to stand committed to the grandame's philosophy of life. When disaster overtook Hobbie, it is a reasonable surmise that no divine will was behind the catastrophe leading him to unhappiness. If we make all the allowances which Scripture and Reason permit, the converse between them in his tearful hours stands out as something noble in its courage, and strong in its simple piety and faith. Scott may sometimes be excused if he do not answer for us our most baffling problems on the enigma of life. The truth is that to keep on the struggle, and yet to find no ultimate answer, is at least one of the ways by which the soul comes to its own. Even Dante, in the profound experience of life and death to which he leads us, has no better resting-place for the human spirit than the assurance, *In voluntate Domini pax nostra est*. This dictum, when closely analysed, is not so far away from the plea of Scott, as it falls from the lips of this Border woman.

Elliot, too, knew how to exhibit the spirit of forbearance to his enemies. To those who have done him ill, even if they are in arms for King James and oppose the Kirk of Scotland that he loves, he will neither make Jacobitism nor Prelacy a ground for division. The lands of Peeblesshire seem to have light cast on them from the country where another Wayfarer trod. If on that far-off land His feet walked with courage, the forgiveness that He showed to His foes knows no distinction of time or place or race. "Just let bygones be bygones and a' freens again," is a sentiment very near the New Testament. There is a good deal in *Black Dwarf* that mirrors the grace of that Book, and that enshrines the Origins of our faith. It has been the fashion of critics to depreciate this tale since the day when Ballantyne offended Scott by his strictures. A careful survey of it reveals hidden beauties to the reader. In any case, when we are in the Borders we seem to be nearer to the spirit of Scott, to the land that he loved, and to the truth that he enshrined.

CHAPTER XV

READERS are familiar with the aversion to his notes which had lingered in Scott's mind when, after consulting a friend as to the value of some manuscript, the writing was estimated at little worth. Then one day he looked over some fishing tackle in a drawer of his desk. The despised literary attempt was observed. It was brought to the light of day, and the task when completed proved to be *Waverley*. This warning to all writers of genius whose worth may not be immediately recognised, ought to be set beside the literary wonder of the *Book of Exeter*. That precious tome, the stores of whose treasures were gathered together at the instigation of Alfred the Great, reached a second edition this year of grace, after thirteen hundred years. English scholars have recently completed that volume for the press, and when it is circulated it may be well to remind ourselves of the discovery of *Waverley*. The two efforts can hardly be set side by side as allied in value. Yet the surprise of the awakened interest, sure though tardy, is an impulse to all workers of merit.

A further personal interest attaches to *Waverley*, as it is generally believed that the introduction not only gives us a transcript of Edward's own career, but that it also forms a fairly minute analysis of the

I

early outlook of the author, his habits of reading, his tastes and dreams. In every detail, of course, it would be unreasonable to trace resemblances. Yet it is well spent time to make a survey of the leading trend in Edward's education if we would better understand the psychology of Walter's developing powers. Teachers, too, may discover in these opening pages material for their data in seeking the origin of real talent, and in explaining to themselves how occasionally in our most developed scholastic system, " the lad o' pairts " seems rather to elude his preceptor. Sometimes he either fails to profit entirely by the wealth of knowledge put at his disposal in the classroom, or he may pursue, as Scott himself often did, his own lines of mental interest, if not in antagonism to his schoolmasters, at least in somewhat diverse lines of enquiry. If we are fully to comprehend the movement of Romanticism in English prose, of which Sir Walter became one of the leaders, if we are even to trace to its source that poetic attitude of mind which helped him to see colour and grace in landscape, and the hidden worth in human life, such an enquiry is inevitable. If we are to follow Edward Waverley in his travels north and south, if we are to share the mood and enter into the spirit of his portrait-painter, then " 'Tis Sixty Years Since " (which is the duplicate title of the book) becomes part of our happy hunting-ground. The youth that is here described is one who learned as he pleased. He had an alertness that resembled intuition. The knowledge which he acquired was not of very solid foundations. He was indolent. His pursuit of any study was not well sustained. He lacked the sense of felicity in expression; he did not possess full concentration. There was something superficial in his relation to learning. It was too lightly thought of. The difficulties of that royal road were not fully faced. Scott well describes Edward as driving "through a sea of books, like a vessel without a pilot or a rudder."

If, as readers of the novels, we are often attracted to the radiance of the by-paths and the high-ways to which our author leads us, we have one secret of it in the love of the youth of Spenser, Milton and Shakespeare. Scott shared also with the young guest at Bradwardine his love of French literature. He revelled in the pages of Froissart, his tales of wars and tournaments. Nevertheless, if there be in some particulars parallels between the young soldier and the coming writer there are also grave differences. Edward was not at home in company as a boy. Scott was the genial fellow-playmate of the boys in Edinburgh High School. The youthful resident at Tullyveolan failed to express what was mentally acquired. He had the information; he could not impart it. Scott on the other hand was even from childhood an inimitable story-teller. Those who sat on the same bench at school with him delighted in the exciting exploits that he had to relate. He had that power so helpful to all who would ultimately arrest the interest of others in the printed page. He had the personality to hold an audience spell-bound. Sometimes we are daring enough to trace this ability of Scott's to those early visits that he paid to the library when his mother imagined that he was sleeping. As little Walter read Elizabethan drama in bed, habits were formed of seeing the glamour in life. He was unconsciously preparing himself for showing us that mystic light upon the pilgrim's way, his own figures in his tales. Many may claim Edward as a duplicate of the juvenile Walter ; and we do not deny the resemblance. Our plea is that in his love of the dramatic situation, in his perception of the appositeness of outward circumstances to throw off the worth of the men and women whom he staged, he is far apart from the hero of *Waverley*. We have only to start with Edward on the journey to the Highlands to discover that the fitness of the locus to the *dramatis personæ* is the result of a mental process for which he was unconsciously training himself. In Scott, it is also another name for genius. He does not only show us the road. He makes us instinctively desire to walk on it along with him, and this Edward Waverley had not the power to do. The gift may be surely more readily acquired in scholastic work. In educational effort to-day is there not a tendency to rest content in the acquisition of data ? Is not the mind made too often only a store-house ? One of the glories of the age to which Scott hel'ped to introduce us is that the really informed person becomes in time a director of others. It is when men are inspired to this idyllic view of life that he has taught us that preachers, poets and artists become possible. To follow Scott's characters not alone within closed doors, but to breathe with them the upland air which his characters inhale, is to unlock one of the secrets of Nature, and to unveil for our fellow-men a Revelation that is in essence divine.

Tullyveolan may be fittingly identified as Grandtully, near Logierait in Perthshire. From Ballinluig a road passes the north bank of the Tay westwards to this village. The Castle of Grandtully dates as far back as 1560. When we visited it, it appeared to reflect much of the stateliness and strength of Bradwardine. Scott, of course, was fond of finding his suggestions for some of his pen-pictures in distant parts of the country, and setting them down in the county associated with his novel, as if the more appropriate edifice could be transposed. If we have ever passed Traquair in Peeblesshire, then the architecture and armorial bearings seem to answer to the description, and that as fittingly as Grandtully Castle on the south bank of the Tay. One peculiar charm makes Traquair as suitable. Since the days of Prince Charlie its gates have been closed. There is a determined purpose in the traditions of the family that only if a Stuart comes again to the throne will they be opened. A section of Traquair is said to be the oldest inhabited house in Scotland. It can be traced to the twelfth century.

In order to get on the true path of *Waverley*, it is better to make Perthshire our starting point. The family crest goes far enough back—" Bewar the Bar ;" it had been granted by an Emperor of Germany for bravery in Palestine.

Edward Waverley finds himself speedily at home in Bradwardine. Scott describes his ready contact with his surroundings, and aptly writes of his eye of blue, " which melted in love and which kindled in war." He had been a captain in the King's army. This sojourn in the Highlands, as well as his association later with Prince Charlie, leads him to espouse the cause of the rebels. There are philosophers

who say that we can rise above our environment.
Edward had not learned that secret. May not
Grandtully Castle be partly the clue to his inde-
cision of character ? The life in that secluded dale
was not sufficiently a challenge for a temperament
such as his. Scott admits that indolence may not
be a vice, but he insists on the unhappiness to which
it may lead. There is no fatalism in the novelist's
standpoint in connecting Edward geographically
with the spot which fails to bring the best out of
him. Nevertheless, if the brief be a reasonable one,
which these Essays seek to elucidate, that there is a
certain inwardness in the ethical effect of environment, then the study of *Waverley* has perhaps deeper
channels of interest than a work of fiction. Is it
idle to surmise what courage and initiative might
have been Edward's, if the shades of this imprisoning
seclusion had not closed about him ?

The author of *Waverley* with Christian humility
envied Maria Edgeworth the vividness of characteri-
sation in her novels. We have discovered
a letter of hers in Hugh Benson's collection,
in which she disclaims any literary superiority to
Sir Walter. It is like his generous heart to seek
to exalt the claims of others. Mr. Andrew Lang
was no easy critic to satisfy. He writes, " When
once we enter the village of Tullyveolan, the
Magician finds his wand. Each picture of place or
person tells. The old butler, the daft Davie Gellatley,
the solemn and chivalrous Baron, the pretty, natural
Flora—the various lairds, the factor Macwheeble,
all at once become living people, and friends whom
we can never lose. The creative fire of Shakespeare lives again."

Scott's friend, Skene, gives verifiable witness to the locus of certain of the great scenes in the tales. After travelling the ground, we have found it of much value to examine Skene's notes. His book was published in 1829, entitled *Sketches of Existing Localities*. He is particularly suggestive in his references to *Waverley*. When Edward was taken prisoner, the reader remembers his approach to the Castle of Doune in Perthshire. Skene records that it was erected at the end of the fourteenth century by the Regent Duke of Albany, the brother of King Robert the Third. Scott poetically describes " this large and massive castle, the half-ruined turrets of which were already glittering in the first rays of the sun." The governor was Donald Stewart, Lieutenant-Colonel in the cause of Prince Charles Edward. Queen Victoria wrote an appreciative letter to a recent Custodian of the Castle for what he had done in writing a sketch of its history. His name is Dunbar, and his book was published in 1886. Doune is memorable to all lovers of *The Scottish Ballads*; and we may still hear under the shadow of the old castle the village children recite the "Bonnie Earl of Moray," with its clinging memories of the tragic past. Edward Waverley was confronted with the iron-grated door of the castle. He was assured of his security, and he fell asleep. It was here he was dispossessed of his papers, and from the courtyard he was mounted next morning and sent forth from the castle with an escort of armed men. The care of the narrator to describe ancient scenes with accuracy is evidenced by the comments of Scott on Doune Castle in the second Volume of *Waverley*.

He writes of how dear it is to his recollection, and of its commanding position on the banks of the river Teith. He tells how the Duke of Albany was beheaded at Stirling on the Castle Hill, and how there he pathetically could behold the towers of Doune—the reminder of the fame from which he had fallen.

It is at Stirling Castle that we now find ourselves in the company of Edward. We recall the Laird of Macwheeble who acted as Captain of the escort that took Waverley from Doune Castle. Scott has this cryptic saying concerning this dissipated soldier. "Balmawhapple with his horse-pistol bids defiance to the artillery of Stirling Castle." As we approach it, the magnificence of its site and its masonry make very apposite the outline that Scott gives of it, the fields where the tournaments were held, the rock from which ladies viewed the conflicts, the towers of the Gothic church. We seem again to see valorous men receive their regal prizes, and to hear the music of the dance and the feast, as gay dames and chivalrous knights passed the hours. We listen again to the roar of the cannon-ball as it rushes over the defiant head of the reckless Balmawhapple.

We find ourselves on the route of these travellers over the field of Bannockburn, through Falkirk, and marching by the old Palace of Linlithgow. We move with them to Edinburgh, and see the piles of Holyrood. We watch the officers of the Palace pass and re-pass. We hear the secretaries at their task of musters and returns. Pitscottie, the old chronicler, writing of the founding of the Palace, has these quaint words : "Thereafter the King cam' to Edinburg, and biggit ane fair palace to himself to repose when he cam' to the toun." These were too perilous days for Prince Charlie to find much repose. The meeting here of Edward Waverley with him, with all the picturesque and historical glamour of the time and the place, makes the interview one of the most striking on the pages of " 'Tis Sixty Years Since." Sir Walter was sufficiently in contact with the period to make it live as a matter of human recollection in the minds of those who had gone through the struggles of the era. We are in the presence of a personality whose voice and manner are now part of the heritage of Scottish life. It is as if in a dialogue of yesterday that we catch the tones of the Prince's winning utterance : " If Mr. Waverley should, like his ancestor Mr. Nigel, determine to embrace a cause which has little to recommend it but its justice, and follow a Prince who throws himself upon the affections of his people to recover the throne of his ancestors, or perish . . . he will follow a master who may be unfortunate, but I trust will never be ungrateful." We remember that the Prince gifted his own broadsword, plated with silver. It was handed over along with his trustful commission to Waverley. These old walls have been the witness of many scenes of thrilling story. In pathos and in colour it would be difficult to rival the hours when Charles Edward cherished his brief dreams of victory, and received the loyal adherence of his followers.

With that fine sense of contrast which so often gives piquancy to Scott's descriptions, this promised glory fades into the dark and irretrievable disaster of Culloden. If we wander out from Inverness to the old battle-field, we can have but one verdict of the power of artful portraiture of the Wizard of the North. He brings us to the glory and the majesty of thrones. As winningly, if more sadly, he pictures to us lost causes, and leaves us with the sense of failure and of tears.

The wanderer at Prestonpans may see the thorn tree, stunted and blighted, which is claimed as the original tree which Sir John Cope made a *point d'appui* in his military affray. It was near this spot that Colonel Gardiner fell. As we look across the fields where Cope was defeated, we can see the Church of Tranent in the distance, which the Highlanders had made their rallying point on the eve of battle. Scott's aptness in weaving with his fiction scenes that are based on solid fact is observed in his portraiture of Colonel Gardiner, a noted Christian and soldier of his day. His deep religious experiences, as well as the impressive nature of his conversion, were noted by Doddridge, the Puritan divine. They form important examples of the concrete doings of an actual personage with whose biography the novelist was familiar. That he should be singled out by Edward Waverley in an hour of danger for his chivalrous help adds interest to his place in history.

Miss Winifred Duke contributed an article on Scott as a Jacobite to *The Quarterly* of April, 1927. She writes with manifest interest in her theme, but does not fully discuss it. She shows that Jacobite blood ran in his veins, and mentions the share of his great-grandfather in Dundee's rebellion. He himself conversed with old men who had known the Prince, and who could not speak of him without tears. Miss Duke, like all Scott's readers, is entranced by his picture of Charles Edward. Yet the glamour of the setting that the novelist gives to the period is not altogether a proof that the Jacobite cause enlisted the novelist's full sympathy. Miss Duke has an incidental comment which reveals a discriminating insight into human nature on her part. She remarks on the quick transfer of Edward's affections. She quaintly finds in the story of the greater hero in *Romeo* a precedent for the romantic transition. Miss Duke's article is worthy of perusal as we read *Waverley*. The period of Prince Charlie's wanderings in Skye has cast a halo round that isle, especially in the north part of Trotternish, which is perhaps not so familiar to tourists as the rest of the misty Isle. Scott alludes to the visit, and his reference stirs the historical student to gain a wide knowledge of the facts, and also to travel the ground. As he passes through Inverness en route, he will reverently stand at the Statue to Flora Macdonald, and will admire the melodious inscription and fine sentiment of the tribute by Samuel Johnson. In 1922, Messrs. Nelson published a volume entitled *A Book of Escapes*. In it is an excellent Essay which embodies the Skye period in Prince Charlie's life. It pictures the landing at Monkstadt with Flora, the suspicion aroused at Lord Macdonald's by the somewhat ungainly Betty Burke, the gallant efforts of his protectors to shield him from peril, his safe deliverance and gratitude to Macdonald, and the wrath of Cumberland's men as they search the isle in vain. Every mile of the ground about the north of Skye is fragrant of Prince Charlie. No one can fail to visit Flora's monument, nor to linger in her old home Flodigarry. If we climb MacLeod's Tables, and look westward to the neighbouring isles and the stormy, dividing seas, we shall marvel the more at the brave girl's heroism, and we shall take the more appreciatively those pages of *Waverley* that recount the doings of the Prince. In Nelson's book there is an excellent map which notes his wanderings, and the pleasure of the tour will be enhanced if the traveller can turn for some hours from " 'Tis Sixty Years Since " and be further won to Skye and its attractions by perusing Boswell's *Journal* and also Seton Gordon's inimitable work, *The Charm of Skye*.

There is a long passage in Scott's *Journal* in which he refers to his visit to Skye. This is another example of the care he took to explore the scenes which he describes, to give the actual locale its true effect on his pages. He was at Dunvegan, and was made familiar with Loch Coruisk. The piper at Abbotsford at one time was a Skyeman. Scott too was an appreciated guest of MacLeod of MacLeod. Unhappily, the scope of this work does not enable us to deal with the fidelity of the artist to places in his Poetry. It may be said in passing that it was a literary revelation to learn from a friend who had been reading *The Lord of the Isles*, and who was a resident in Skye familiar with all the ground, how closely detailed are Scott's descriptions, how place and spirit are made twin sisters in his grouping of the scenic features. In his *Journal*, he writes of Loch Scavaig, which we cross on our way to Coruisk. It is suggestive to discover Mr. Seton Gordon in a more recent Essay urging his readers to turn again to that poem of Scott's for the visualising of the scenes. Certainly *The Lord of the Isles* is a fitting companion to *Waverley*, if we would sail to the haunts made attractive to us in the book. If the visitor go by Elgol to Loch Coruisk, he will travel past a landing-stage in the journeys of the Prince.

Nothing in the story of the '45 is more fragrant than the unselfish devotion of followers to the losing cause. Scott brings us to the thought of which St. Paul and Browning were such rich interpreters, that the hope unrealised, the dream not fulfilled are working for us " a far more exceeding weight of glory." We feel this as we visit Carlisle. It brings us to the dawn of that morning when Edward Waverley stood in front of the old Gothic gate of the Castle. . . . " I was only ganging to say, my Lord," said Evan Dhu, " that if your excellent honour and the honourable Court would let Vich Ian Vohr go free just this once, and let him gae back to France, and no to trouble King George's government again, that ony six o' the very best of his clan will be willing to be justified in his stead ; and if you'll just let me gae doun to Glennaquoich, I'll fetch them up to ye mysell, to heid or hang, and you may begin wi' me the very first man." The place where Fergus was imprisoned had out-works dating back to the period of Henry the Eighth. Even to-day it is a weird spot to enter. Its thick walls, its isolation from human fellowship, the darkness of its dungeons stir thoughts of pity. There is an irony, too, in the remembrance that MacIvor and Maccombich ere they went to execution could look across the Border, and think of the hills of home. For them the crowning sorrow was as they recalled their defeated purpose to lead their Prince to the throne.

When we entered these dark regions where the Scottish Highlanders waited for execution, we were surprised to find on the stone walls work of rare artistry. It bore the evidence of skilled chiselling, and it embodied the designs of rare Egyptian hieroglyphics. Had any one of them seen service in the East? Was theirs that enviable gift of mental detachment by which their days of endurance were lightened as they employed their exceptional gifts? At all events, the walls are a testimony to their patient labour. They are more; they are a suggestion of some yearning for a higher power than earth could yield them, as they met their doom. The Prince was no longer there to inspire them. Their trust went higher. On the walls there is still enshrined the Cross of Christ. If Scott avers that the last words that Fergus uttered were "God save King James," it was on an arm more divine than that of the dynasty of Stuart that he and his comrade greeted the unseen. Perhaps, in these days we sit too lightly to the sentiment that binds us to "place." In our national traditions, home and the surroundings that love has hallowed are bound in a link so firm that nothing can sever them, at least from adoring remembrance. When we are called to break the tie, we seem to leave part of ourselves behind. In days such as Scott describes the servant and retainer were bound almost as strongly in tender regard to the walls as were the family. There are few more beautiful instances of the novelist's pride of proprietorship, the wedding of spirit to stone and lime and garden, than in the closing Act of *Waverley*. Janet Gellatley, that faithful attendant of the Bradwardines, rejoices that Tullyveolan is regained by her master, despite his affecting the lost cause of Stuart. Edward Waverley wished to recompense her for her fidelity. " How can I be rewarded, sir, sae weel," she answers, " as just to see my auld maister and Miss Rose come back, and bruik their ain ? "

The pages of Lockhart, the closing scenes in Winifred E. Gunn's play where Tom Purdie serves his beloved Sir Walter as if he never left Abbotsford, show how love of home was intertwined with the best in the novelist's own life. There is an old song which left its refrain in his spirit. " This is no mine ain hoose, I ken by the biggin o' it." This attachment of his is one of the forgotten factors in the development of the *genius loci* which are so manifestly instanced on the pages of *Waverley*.

CHAPTER XVI

A LEGEND OF MONTROSE
THE LENY PASS, PERTHSHIRE, AND ARGYLL

If we would enter into the spirit of this tale, it should be our eager task to pass up the Leny Pass from Callander, with its overshadowing hill above us. We shall find ourselves in Menteith, which is part of the region which this novel covers. If we make our way to Lochearnhead, we shall be within reach of Ardvorlich House. The road on the south shore of Loch Earn passes it. It was at Ardvorlich that Macgregor craved hospitality from the forester's sister, and then presented to her her brother's head. We are within some miles of Glen Ample, where there is an old Castle of the Bredalbanes. To the south of the house stands Ben Voirloch.

It is on the pass to Leny that the introduction of the book ushers us. Here we have the meeting between Lord Menteith and Dugald Dalgetty. Montrose put much confidence in Menteith, and he was one of his friends. Menteith later joined in the campaign. When Scott describes him, he writes, " There was conspicuous in him a flash of the generous, romantic, disinterested chivalry of the old heroic times." Dalgetty had been a student of Marischal College, Aberdeen. He became a soldier, and in all the services of Europe he was known as *bonus socius*. He became a captain in the army of Montrose. In a spirit of patriotism he had come to Scotland in the hour of her peril. After the battle of Inverlochy he was knighted. Montrose called him a man of the times. He was resourceful and alert, but of an over-ready tongue. Menteith cannot at first understand how it is that Dalgetty manages to satisfy his conscience when being so willing to fight either for Royalist or Whig. Dalgetty had told him " Whilk cause is best I cannot say." The Captain's eye he confessed was for the side on which he would be most gratefully rewarded.

If we take the road by Loch Earn, which has been described, we reach Ardvorlich. The ancient house was burnt down, and the one at present standing does not go back nearly to the seventeenth century period on which Scott dilates. It is certainly worth seeing, not only because it is on the land associated with thrilling deeds in that era, but because its arms and military weapons take us into the atmosphere that the novelist so vividly presents to us. When Lord Menteith and Dalgetty saw it, it stood in land more wooded than it now is. The branches of the trees gleamed red at sunset, and formed one of those pictures which Scott in a few lines knew so well how to paint. He portrays its bartizans, turrets and courtyard, the loop-holes for its musketry and its surrounding wall, its windows secured by stanchions of iron. Dugald tramped into the stable, refusing help for his beloved horse Gustavus. The Laird of Darnlinvarach was Angus McAulay. He was one of the leaders of the Highlanders of Montrose. What led him to this he never could tell. In reply to Sir Duncan

Campbell, he could only say that " the iron hand of destiny branded our fate upon our forehead long ere we could form a wish, or raise a finger in our own behalf." The younger brother was called Allan. He was shy, impatient and morose. A fierce contest was waged between the McAulays of Darlinvarach and the MacEaghs, the Children of the Mist. These MacEaghs wandered amongst the mountains and glens. The McAulays' uncle on their mother's side had been murdered, according to the story which is familiar to all readers of the book. The Children of the Mist were savage and vindictive. They had never experienced the life of well-ordered men. Ronald MacEagh eventually destroyed the Castle of Ardenvohr which belonged to Sir Duncan Campbell. Campbell was a friend of Menteith and of the McAulays. Argyle sent him to Darlinvarach to attempt to stay the Highland rising. He was not successful, but he fought bravely, and was wounded at Inverlochy by Ronald MacEagh. Scott has described him in a sentence : " Brave in war, honest in peace, and true in council." We shall look forward to meeting him in Inverary Castle ; and we must not at this stage forecast the stirring events which meet us in Argyllshire. It was he who stirred the enmity of Allan to Menteith. Scott has a comprehensive chapter at the beginning of his book in which he treats of the state of Scotland during the Civil War. There had departed at that time to England the Scottish army under the Earl of Leven. In the summer of 1644, James Grahame, Marquis of Montrose, travelled into the Highlands incognito. He had with him the mandate of Charles the First, to command the Royalists. We are led through the battles at Tippermuir, Aberdeen and Inverary. We are brought to Inverlochy in Inverness-shire, where Montrose's triumph was reached on 2nd February, 1645. Anderson is the name which Montrose assumed when he was in disguise in the Highlands; and it is in this character we find him chatting with the men at Darlinvarach. This is one of many reasons why it is of such unforgettable value to wander round the old castle near Loch Earn, and to feel the impress of " the Great Marquis " upon us. It was during General Leslie's absence in England that he raised the royal standard. There are certain reasons assigned for his success, his powerful personality, and his deep-seated enmity against the House of Argyle which the Highland clans shared. He had also the help of an Irish supporting party. Scott says of him, " his soul looked through his eyes with all the energy and fire of genius." There is a picturesqueness and appeal in Scott's opening for us the door of the Castle and permitting us to mingle with the Royalist leader, as in the assumed habit of Lord Menteith's servant he mingles with the company and drinks of the country ale. We can see in the dark-vaulted vestibule the frown on the face of the Highland menial, as Anderson with a nicety not too common in the kitchen of Darlinvarach flings out the drop of ale (which remains in the wooden cup) and rinses it. There is not much that escapes the eye of Sir Walter. If he rises to magnificence in his treat-ment of great events, he has the artist's genius for bringing to light the minor deed. Pitt remarked when he had read some of his writing that this was the kind of thing he expected in painting, but never thought possible in writing. Quiller Couch once asked his students at Cambridge, why Samuel Johnson with all his perversity lives to-day? His reply was in a single phrase : " He never saw literature but as a part of life, nor would he allow in literature what is false to life, as he saw it." There is something in the literary honesty of Johnson which closely resembles the ingenuousness of Scott.

Darlinvarach Castle gains an added interest from the sound of music within its walls, and the figure of Annot Lyle. Browning's *Saul* gives us a fine study of the influence of harmony on a mind dejected. The picture that Scott has drawn of this melodist must be placed beside it. That is a striking scene in the Castle when Lord Menteith meets Allan McAulay, and they discuss the song which Annot gives them accompanied by her harp. " Thank God," exclaims Allan, " my soul is no longer darkened ; the mist has passed from my spirit."

Then in a swift transition, so frequent in these novels, we are presented to another phase of the activity of Darlinvarach—the arrival of the Highland Chiefs, " all plaided and plumed in their tartan array," as Lochiel happily phrases it. Lord Menteith explains that they are met to throw off the rebels of the King, and to manifest their revolt at the Earl of Leven's incursion into England. Then after discussion, an aged man reminds the assembled band that it is not strength alone that wins the fight, but the head of the commander. Alister More depicts the type of leader that they require, wise, brave, skilful. It is a dramatic moment in the Castle when McAulay lays his hand upon the shoulder of Anderson and cries, " Here he stands." When we visit Darlinvarach, we seem to have in front of us again the parchment which Anderson presented to the gathering, and to hear anew, as they did in his tones, the voice of Grahame, Earl of Montrose. There echoes within these walls the sayings of Coriolanus : " Then were they chosen. In a better hour, Let what is meet be said."

We do not know whether that " better hour " has come. In any case, this is not the place in which to analyse the motives that led to the selection of Montrose, nor is it the time in which to comment on Scott's treatment of him. There is ground for the belief held by able historians that a glamour is cast upon his figure which (while largely justified, as the description of a military hero), scarcely does justice to the true greatness of Argyle. Lord Macaulay, in no measured terms, revealed his views from that more balanced view of history. It has been pointed out, too, that while Scott leaves us with the triumph of Montrose lingering in our mind, he does not carry us beyond this to the sequel of that great career not so glorious. Much of the zest of the Royalist party, especially amongst the Highlanders, was due to animus against Argyle not always just. It is only right to quote Macaulay, who remarks that " of all the Highland princes whose history is well known to us, he is the greatest." At Inverlochy this historian had the chance to hear from Highlanders about the doings of the 1645 rebellion. He was interested to discover that with a fine

loyalty to the noble house of Argyle they did not
describe it as a reversal for him or his troops, but
rather as " the victory of the Macdonalds over the
Campbells."

If the visitor to the great scenes in *The Legend of
Montrose* wish detailed data he cannot do better
than consult the researches of Skene. He has
interesting notes both on Inverlochy and on Ardenvohr ; the latter he identifies with Dunstaffnage.
As we view these old sites, the words of Butler seem
to be wafted on the air.

> " Such do build their faith,
>   Upon the holy text of pike, and gun."

Since Skene's day, workers' dwellings have been
built on the battlefield of 1645. Inverlochy lies
a mile north from Fort William, which overlooks
Loch Linnhe. Ben Nevis lifts its giant-like form
above us, as if it had never been the witness to
desperate hours of war.

Sir Walter has a charming manner in odd
moments of confessing his whims. He tells us
frankly in one of his essays that he is sometimes
led off his main road over hedges and ditches when
some whimsical character is being weaved in his
fancy. He mentions, as an instance, the figure of
Dugald Dalgetty. If Scott be led off the main track
in his novel by him, may the reader be blamed if his
doings lead him also to journeys far from Darlinvarach ? As we motored one summer from Angus to
Aberdeen, on approaching that city our thoughts
dwelt on Drumthwacket. Readers recall how the
facetious soldier boasted sometimes of that estate.

A Legend of Montrose

Sibbald described it as a long, waste moor, five miles south of the city. We seemed to hear again Dugald's angry tones as he gave his opinion to Sibbald of the Covenanter who was reputed lately to have purchased his estate. Dalgetty claimed that in his own family it had remaind for four hundred years. But when we visit Old Aberdeen and picture him as a Latin scholar there, we wistfully wonder whether the gallant band that now throng the old quadrangle imbibe as gaily in war and in peace Dugald's unceasing devotion to the Latin tongue !

We followed his shades at all events to the Castle of Inverary. Through the kindness of the present Duke of Argyle, we were able the more readily to listen to Dugald's voice, and to discover the setting of his gloomy sojourn in the old dungeon there. He was sent, we recall, as an emissary of Montrose to that famous Castle. Scott is always happiest in his dramatic scenes, when he introduces them in the *locus* that he has actually known. His acquaintance with the surroundings is all too familiar to readers of the *Legend* to justify quotations. We recollect his picture of Loch Fyne, the fine minuteness of scenic effect, as he paints the rival rivers Aray and Achray, which flow into the loch from their wooded retreat. At that time the water crept right up to Inverary, and the landing was as described in the approach of Dugald to this ancestral home of the Argyles.

There seems to us to be little need of Burns's sad epigram on his visit. For, after all, there is a deference due to an old family, and for once perhaps the poet may have not quite realised the part which genius may pay to honour and arms. The interview

151

with the Son of the Mist, the clever overtures with
the Duke's Chaplain, which perhaps only an
Aberdonian can accomplish with Dugald's con-
summate art, the escape, Ronald's relation of his
tale of Annot Lyle remain as precious treasures
of these inimitable hours. The passage through the
town, the sight of the gibbets, as they rode, the
journey over the mountains of the north, bring
us, as all Scott's best work does, to the hour and to
the place. The reader may be pardoned, if after
lingering over the book, he employs Montrose's
lines in tribute to the teller of this tale, that W. S.
Crockett ranks as the most excellent of the
Waverleys.

> " I'll serve thee in such noble ways,
>   As ne'er were known before ;
> I'll deck and crown thy head with bays,
>   And love thee more and more."

Scott's interpreters trace the impulse which created
Dugald Dalgetty to the author's knowledge of
Sir James Turner. There is much resemblance
between them. It is suggestive to find Sir James in
his Memoirs uttering a sentiment which might have
come as appropriately from the pen of Dugald—" I
have swallowed without chewing in Germanie a
very dangerous maxim which military men there too
much follow : which was that so we serve our
master honestlie, it is no matter what master we
serve." We admit that the ethic of this saying is
defective. Yet almost as winningly as the strains
of Annot's harp move us, these words bring us
nearer to Dalgetty. We stand with him again in

A Legend of Montrose

Inverary and in Darlinvarach, and as we listen to the sonorous sentence—has not Dugald translated it into Latin, and does he not relate to us again the doings of the college in Aberdeen ? Is it possible to appreciate Sir Walter unless like him we sometimes wander from the highway and take men such as Dalgetty as our companions on the path ?

CHAPTER XVII

THE devotee of Scott will make his way to Luce
Abbey, where Lochinvar has his resting-place.
Nine miles from Castle Kennedy he will pass
Glenluce, near which the Abbey lies. From the
village of Glenluce he will visit Carsreugh Castle,
which is the reputed early home of the Bride of
Lammermoor. In this house the wedding of Lady
Ashton took place. The wedding contract of the
historic prototype in the Dalrymple family is
amongst the Selkirk papers and is signed at
Carsreugh. It is a somewhat perplexing problem in
the analysis of this novel that such different Counties
are involved. The background of the earlier section
of the book differs from the latter. We are trans-
ported from Wigtownshire to East Lothian. The
reason is not far to seek. Scott must have been
partly guided by the suitability of the different
Counties to unveil more dramatically his tragical
plot. It is a proof of the influence 'place' had upon
him. It is the evidence that graphic and vital as
his portraitures of human life are, part of their
magnetism is due to land and sea. These their
grandeur makes more revealing—the deep internal
issues which the characters themselves reveal. It
has been said with truth that *The Bride of Lammer-*

moor is on the literary level of Greek tragedy. Every student of Sophocles, Euripides and the rest finds there also the same alliance. In his *Introduction to Medea*, Professor Gilbert Murray admits that Medea, despite "its background of wonder and enchantment, is not a romantic play but a tragedy of character and situation." To find a word expressive of the union of the inward situation with the outward is not easy. The Greeks had a phrase Κατ᾿ ἦθος Λέγεσθαι. It is used, e.g., in the *Rhetoric* of Aristotle. It came near the idea of a moral impression, and Philostratus applies it in this sense when writing of a statue. There is a union also between the physical and the spiritual which makes the soul shine through the eye, or reveal itself in some gesture. Scott has the power to make the character of his figures display itself in the mere description of their appearance. This is a cognate idea on which future writers may well plan their work. How the artist in words accomplishes it is another question. Edmund Spenser penned lines which, in such a work as this, form part of the inspiration of our task.

> "Now of the soul, the body form at first did take,
>   For soul *is* form, and doth the body make."

This power of portraiture is revealed all through the novel. To give instances would be merely to rehearse what the reader must often have observed. Scott has done this service in all the characters of the tale. "Edgar's morbid outlook quenched the light and ingenuous vivacity of youth in a countenance singularly fitted to display both." Sir William

Ashton is described as "a cool lawyer and able politician." His wife is summed up in the epithets —"proud, vindictive and predominating." Lucy is borne along by the will of others, "with as little power of opposition as the flower which is flung into a running stream." Craigenfelt could "hoist any colours at a pinch." We find this revealing power of the novelist in the tenderness of the Revd. Bide-the-Bent, on the eve of the wedding, and in Caleb's grief on the death of his master, which we shall interpret later in this chapter. " His life," says Scott, " lost its salt and its savour."

There are few of the Waverley novels where the spirit of the drama casts its light more clearly through the local surroundings. A mile or two from Wigtown stand the ruins of Baldoon. This was the home of Bucklaw. The traveller would almost imagine that there was a blight on the place. Almost nothing remains of any importance in the ruin. There still may be seen the chastely carved gateway through which Lucy would have passed after the fatal bridal day if she had survived. Her brother, on the day of the wedding, as he rode, felt Lucy's hand. The coldness as of marble in the fingers of the bride alarmed him. On the old marriage schedule we can still see the marks of that cold, trembling hand in the shaky penmanship. When we are at Wigtown we look over the waters of Blednoch. One of the Covenanting women, who was drowned there in the persecuting days, was brought to her trial through the information of the same clergyman who conducted the service on Lucy's wedding-day. There is historical evidence that this Mr. Simpson held the incumbency of the neighbouring church at Kirkinner. Surely an unexpected light falls on his character when we recall that he and Margaret McLachlan were contemporaries, and that he was an informant against her.

In Wigtown, certainly, we are in the countryside that is reminiscent of the episodes of the unfortunate marriage. There were friends of Sir Walter's that were acquainted with happenings in an old family of that county, the records of which in many ways resemble those that the novelist describes. The somewhat lonely district would naturally give rise to the introspection and self-analysis which would be easily encouraged in the heart of Lucy. She loved Ravenswood. To him she had plighted her troth. They had each possessed themselves in that solemn tryst of a little band of gold. She wore hers constantly tied with blue ribbon. Through the machinations of Sir William, her father, and under the dominant control of Lady Ashton, her mother, she was released of her promise to Ravenswood. His letters to her were intercepted. The time-limit fixed for his supposed admission that Lucy would be no longer his was fixed for St. Jude's day. As she heard the sound of his horse's hoofs on his return to this country to claim her, she realised all too poignantly that she had been deceived, and that the report of his alliance to another maiden was false. A recent interpreter of the book gives another instance in the tale when the sound of horse's hoofs is heard. It is the scene in the churchyard when the impression is one of tense emotion. In his comment, he ranks the passage with the knocking in *Macbeth*. Glenluce Church is reputed to be the place of the bridal ceremony. Carsreugh, Lucy's early home in the neighbourhood, was the natural centre of hospitality after the wedding. That part of the County is associated with the tale, and that Kirkinner, whose minister wrote an elegy (which still may be read) after Lucy's death, is in proximity, gives a further link with that district. We are here under the shadow of Castle Kennedy. It is within that family circle that much of the thrill of these days of war, romance and peril can be traced.

> " 'Tween Wigtown and the toun o' Ayr,
>   Portpatrick and the Cruives o' Cree,
> No man need think for to bide there,
>   Unless he court with Kennedie."

There are various theories as to the authentic site of Ravenswood. We do not propose to balance the pros and cons of each plea. We have explored several of them and been impressed by the weight of arguments for all. Suffice it to say that in that learned work of W. S. Crockett, *The Scott Originals*, careful scrutiny is given of several. We do not wish to rehearse again the matter which he has so ably handled. It appears a mistaken view in too detailed analysis to commit Scott to any particular *locus* where such might be open to question. Dr. Crockett is an unprejudiced surveyor. The reader is referred to his pages. The brief which we seek to hold is not one of geographical identification. It is rather to convince the student of the novels, that while imaginative flights keep him spellbound, yet repeatedly he may find his feet on Mother Earth. He may entertain himself by the happy surmise that certain localities lend themselves more than others to the treatment Scott gives them. If he peruse his *Journal* he will often find corroborating evidence that the author *has* been in places which seem conclusively to mirror the loveliness of earth and which depict the architecture and setting of dwellings in the tale. The visitor to Palestine is more concerned in gaining that sense of the realism of Scripture events than of dogmatically assigning sites to places which are only rooted to traditional authority. Is not this feeling of contact with Wigtownshire apparent in *The Bride of Lammermoor*? Is it not more than evident in delineation of East Lothian? Is there not a symmetry in the pages of Scott similar to what we find in Chaucer? In her comments on that fourteenth-century poet, Miss Grace Hadow of Oxford has a cognate passage on Cressida. As we read it, we seem to find a replica of the portrait of Lucy Ashton in Scott. " We realise Cressida's beauty," she writes, " rather from the effect it produces on others than from any particular details ; . . . the strong impression which she undoubtedly produces is due to Chaucer's power of creating an atmosphere rather than to actual description. We hear the nightingale singing her to sleep, or watch her colour come and go as Troilus draws near, and our mind is so filled with an image of youth and beauty that we never stop to think if she is fair or dark."

On the south-east of Scotland the traveller from the south of Berwick is familiar with St. Abb's Head. To the west of this lies Fast Castle. It is tempting to find in this the suggestive ruin which gave Scott his idea of Wolf's Crag. Sam Bough's painting of the Crag is certainly very similar to that of Scott's description. It is approached by a little narrow bridge, and it looks out on the stormy ocean. It stands on a position of great advantage for defence and yet it is in touch with the scattered homes on the coast-line. The scene in *The Bride of Lammermoor*, when Edgar entertains Sir William and Lucy, comes vividly back to memory. Visitors to the Victoria and Albert Gallery will recall that work of W. P. Frith in which he depicts their meeting. We hear in imagination the echoes of the thundering knocks on the old gate when the hunting party arrived. We share Caleb Balderstane's consternation at the poverty of his larder. The loyal adherent of Martensen's ethical views can hardly excuse his subterfuges as he conceals the state of the provisions of the house. Yet we cannot in much amusement refrain from admiring his devoted loyalty to his master, his desire to shield him from blame as an ungenerous host, his willingness to do anything within his power to put a good face upon an awkward domestic predicament. Ravenswood, with its wide parks and fruitful fields, has within its bounds no more faithful retainer than Caleb. The care with which he tended him in hours of safety and watched over him in peril is portrayed by Scott with full knowledge of the allegiance of a man to his master when he is trusted and left unhampered in his tasks. The author is sometimes unjustly charged with allowing the attitude of the aristocrat to obscure in his mind the needs of social reform. Scott's policy in relation to many of the inequalities of his day was not through political reconstruction but through the influence of individual lives. Part of his creed as a philanthropist was that high ethical relationships between class and class form part of the solution of our economic problems. In our own century it is of course not possible to solve our present national problems by so simple and so unofficial an action and reaction. At the same time, we have a feeling after reading such books as *Christianity and the present Moral Unrest* that by stressing the administrative aspect of social reform, there is at least a danger of ignoring the more inward and spiritual relationship. If there are fewer Caleb Balderstanes to-day, then perchance Wolf's Crag has not fully left the impress of its lesson on the more fevered life of this era. Where may devotion to a family whom he served, and to a master whom he loved, be more tenderly portrayed than in the closing scene of all, when Ravenswood is lost in the sand with the incoming tide ? A critic has aptly said that there is more poetry in the epilogue of the book than in any piece of prose that Scott wrote.

Those who frequent that rugged east coast and who visualise the setting, will readily find the last act in that tragedy reappear before the imagination. The duel has been arranged between Caleb's master and Colonel Ashton. As the waiting opponent rides along, he sees the figure of Ravenswood suddenly sink into the enshrouding sand. It has been driven by the swiftly oncoming tide. The brave horseman, the disappointed lover, is plunged to his fate. Scott tells how only one vestige of his doom appears,—a large sable feather. The waves, as they rippled in the morning air, carried it to Caleb's feet.

Scott and the Lure of the Road

It is here that place and soul—the one so awesome, the other so bewildered—are woven so finely together. Scott in his Introduction refrains from fixing on Fast Castle as the Wolf's Crag of the tale. He had only seen it himself from the sea. He admits that this promontory is as like the projecting crag and castle which he has pictured as any other. He allows for the nearness of the ridge of Lammermoor, which the observer may readily trace in the map, as a likely locus for these fatal hours. The point to stress is not to insist on mere identity. It is rather to assess the æsthetic worth of the author's use of his material, and above all his aptness in throwing off to the best effect on his canvas the spiritual worth of love and other treasures that time and earth cannot dim. " If worldly profit could have consoled the old man," says Scott, " his age was better provided for than his earlier years had ever been." His whole course of ideas, his feelings, whether of pride or of apprehension, of pleasure or of pain, had all arisen from his close connection with the family which was now extinguished. He ate without refreshment and slumbered without repose."

Mr. Buchan regards *The Bride of Lammermoor* as the most perfectly constructed of the Waverley novels. His estimate is that never did Scott write better prose than in his description of Wolf's Crag. This view is not an isolated piece of criticism. Lockhart put it *facile princeps*. In his canons of value he emphasized its purity and its strength. It is of incomparable interest to the student to go over the ground both in East Lothian and in Wigtownshire with a map. There is a realism in the mental effort to bring the book within the compass of the fair landscape, the ever-changing sea, the floating cloudland with which Nature crowns her places of beauty.

For earth is one of the elemental forces in life. In touch with it as in contact with grave human needs, it is not possible for man to be insincere. He feels that his one means of preserving his soul is to allow the awe and the loveliness of the world which God has made to reflect something of the light and darkness, the hope and the terror of his own struggling soul. In this book the profound things of life stand out with majesty. The simple happenings own a lustre as of other worlds. We appear to touch the hem of a garment not of our own fashioning. It is as if the earth became the outer garment of the Unseen. Something akin to this the Hebrew poets enshrine in their finest lyrics. They gave it a spiritual significance. For them the earth was the Lord's and the fullness thereof.

CHAPTER XVIII

THE MONASTERY—AND MELROSE ABBEY

IF *The Monastery* is to prove for us an attraction, then in our thoughts we do well to set it in the midst of the moving events of history where the story has its birth. The battle of Pinkie had been fought. Its tale was unforgettable, leaving behind it its harvest of sorrow. Mary of Lorraine and Cardinal Beaton were strong forces in the defence of Romanism. Their policy was naturally opposed to that of England, for Protestantism was an impulse of power in the national life south of the Tweed. Scotland, through the Reformation had shown its kinship with the fresh light and learning which enlightened Churchmen who had studied at European centres of culture were bravely disseminating. The seeds of the pure Evangel were being scattered. The fruition was not as yet all for which eager hearts hoped. The abbeys and monasteries were in a state of unrest. The revolt against the teaching of the Church that they represented was sufficiently evidenced to make their patrons tremble for the future. We are debtors to Scott for bringing us in this novel to a more balanced sense of the period of transition from the old faith to the new. The reading of Scottish history in periods that have given rise (as the Reformation has done) to convulsion and to tumult, is apt to yield merely the impression that this great event was the

end of an old era and the miraculous commencement
of a new. To a certain extent this is true. If,
however, this be the extent of our historical rehearsal,
then ours is a very inadequate analysis. The roots
of the ancient Creed of Rome went very deep. The
religious Renaissance had hardly full time to
express itself without prejudice on the one side or
the other. Whenever a cataclysm occurs in spiritual
affairs, it leaves the marks of upheaval, bitterness,
and even of enmity. It is one of the services that
Scott has done to the understanding of the
period, that he shows the immediate issues of that
conflict. He beckons us as it were within the circle
of religious men of the period. We learn to see
the struggle, as all conflict must be seen, from
within. We admire the strength and fervour of
saints of the type of Henry Warden, whose work
was like the coming of spring to a winter of discontent. We are surprised that Mr. Buchan has
not a higher estimate of Scott's analysis of that
really strong character. When we reach the Castle
of Avenel, we shall consider Warden more fully.
To souls of such piety, resourcefulness and courage,
we never can be other than debtors. This admission must never obscure from us the fact that though
mixed with error, Romanism had been the conser-
vator of much that an enlightened age is apt in a
measure to lack. We have only to turn to Harnack's
History of Monasticism, or to the work of Foakes
Jackson, to learn the worth of music, art and letters
that such ancient houses secured. Beauty in
worship, punctilious devotion to the routine of
spiritual exercises, toil in manual tasks, and the
development of such stately architecture that even

in its ruins is the envy of all souls who are incited to grace by outward loveliness—these are some of the dowries which it would be unchristian to leave without acknowledgment. Beauteous border towns still unhappily bear the painful effects on fair buildings of the raids of the Earl of Hertford. It is only fair to recall this. The destruction of the best was not all due to Puritanical zeal, nor to revolt at what is beautiful in worship. It is well, therefore, that the pilgrim who studies *The Monastery* walk also within the sacred aisles of Melrose Abbey. For it is here that the locus of the novel is found. This is the original of his St. Mary's. He calls it Kennaquhair. The word comes from Quhair, the winding course of a stream='Ken n'a' where'? "I don't know where." All who visit Melrose, and who look on the river from the heights above it, recall the ser-pentine form of that silver stream. The Abbey was founded by David the Sair Sanct of Scotland. Does it not say much for the enterprise of the Church of the day that the light of this holy place should be set here amid the things of darkness? We may yield to none in our adherence to the Creed which is embodied in our Confessions. We may at the same time, and with equal sincerity, admit that the deliverance which the ancient Church gave to the community by the foundation of this Abbey was as great a release from bondage as the services of our Reformation champions who safeguarded for us the Evangel which we prize.

Such things require to be said, if we would truly feel our debt to Sir Walter, and if we would fully appreciate the colour and life which he gives to the era which *The Monastery* opens out for us. In any interpretation of his work, it is never sufficient merely to mark the fitness of his tale to its geographical setting. It is equally needful to dovetail the story in its narrower events into the history of the land whose future and worth are bound up with it. In greater detail, we have already sought to do this in *Black Dwarf*. It is as important, however briefly, to mark a like sense of balance in this novel. The Sixteenth Century movement is rightly assessed by Scott. It was a re-interpretation of doctrines which had grown corrupted. If we praise the work of the reformers, and if we wish to re-discover the glory of Melrose Abbey, this will not be the reward of a mere pilgrimage to it. In our study of its records we must not grudge our homage to men of saintly life who led men from the wilderness of ignorance into the fold. Such, e.g., was Father Ambrose, the last Abbot of St. Mary's. Scott shows that " in the days of her tribulation, which had rent asunder the allegiance of Christians to the Church, he was turned out of home and homestead, and deprived of the temporalities of that noble house of God." This is a valued plea for studying *The Monastery* with the sense of the historical background. Principal Lindsay has shown in his *History of the Reformation* that it was the sacred songs sung over Europe by men of the piety of Ambrose, that prepared the hearts of the nations for redemption. It was in the sanctuaries and homes of the followers of Rome that these harmonies were heard.

In our advocacy of the fitness of the setting of Scott's tales, we have a fine illustration in Melrose itself. The country that lies around it is redolent of loveliness. Earth and Heaven have become one texture of beauty. These walls appear the picture of peace. The spiritual jewel has a fine setting. When the by-gone traveller, sore beset, caught sight of it, its inviting guest-chamber was kept open in the long hours of darkness. Music was heard within it, the plaintive chanting of the psalter as the monks performed their musical tasks. The Scriptorium had its store of parchments. Gifted children such as the Glendinnings gained the benefit of such education as the brethren had time or ability to bestow. The soil was cultivated with unstinted care. In this twentieth century the Church of Scotland in portions of its "vineyard" is emulating the work on the land that these old religious houses cultivated. In its social reform it is leading idle men to allotted ground as these Christian votaries did in the era Scott has described. By the employment of their hands in spade and in garden-culture it is making the Church a more real factor in their lives. Our more progressive Parliamentarians on a much larger scale are setting their minds to give tasks to unemployed men. Our present political advisers find their leading motive, not in any utilitarian scheme nor commercial venture, but in the deepening of the sense of the nation's morale.

Scott has done for us another service in the disclosure to us of such homes of sanctity. He makes us realise the better how large a factor loveliness that meets the eye may be in people's lives. Those windows of priceless beauty, the double piscina in the chancel, the scrupulous workmanship, leave their impress on the reader of *The Monastery* to-day.

They wed for him the items of outward richness to the enduring things of inward worth.

In the workmanship of his structure, the reader finds full warrant for Scott's allusions. We may possibly feel that the White Lady of Avenel is a somewhat fantastic personage. The episode may have its humorous aspects in the adventure of the sacristan, and his icy plunge in the water. If this be so, its introduction to the tale serves a useful purpose. It directs our attention to the old customs of the bridges of that time. The burn was the Elwan. The bridge on which the dictatorial Peter was guardian was a little below the confluence of that stream and the Tweed. At one time, it was possible when the bridge had been demolished to see the pillars. By 1772 these had gone. One traveller describes one which he had seen about a mile or two from Melrose. In one of the towers there was a resident custodian who laid planks from pillar to pillar, and conveyed passengers across. It was the obstinacy of the bridge-keeper of his day that landed the sacristan in his perils by water.

> " I see the Abbey, both turret and tower,
>   Is all astir for the vesper hour;
>   The monks for the chapel are leaving each cell,
>   But where's Father Philip should toll the bell ? "

The episode, absurd as it may seem, introduces us to the collision of thought which at that time was so marked between the devotee of the breviary and mass, and the reader of the Scripture. The Bible had been brought over from the Continent amid the cargo. It had been hidden behind the bales of cotton. In such quiet homes as Glendearg, which we visited on the hillside, it was beginning to be pondered and read. By the dramatic way in which the discovery was made by the monk of Lady Avenel's black volume with the silver clasp, we are brought vividly to a sense of the freshness of the truth that it disclosed to these shores. Scott's antiquarian studies may have convinced him of the worth of ritual and missal. His strong cogitative nature made him very much alive to the loss the Medieval Church had sustained through the denial of the Scripture to its adherents. There are passages in *The Monastery* which bring home to us the exhilarating power that comes to simple and wise alike in the reading of these writings too long denied them. It is on record that there was discovered in St. Mary's a translation of the Scriptures in the vulgar tongue. In a secluded recess it was found. This event appears to bring us into very close contact with Sir Walter's survey. He knew too well the bitterness of days when the Book was under ban. It was said of Halbert " that he loved the lance and the sword more than the good text and holy word." Mary Avenel in an hour of grief lifts the board in the flooring. She finds the Book which her mother loved. This scene gives a local touch to the conflict which waged at the period over the introduction of Scripture to the people. She was ignorant of its contents. Her kinswoman had inserted slips of paper within the pages beside favourite passages. These helped her in her hour of need. The circulation of truth in quiet ways such as this brought Romanism spiritual reverses. Men and women began to enquire for themselves into the tenets of their religion. With the stirring

of their interest and their imagination came the
birth of freedom, and the stirring of a new conscience. It is because of these permeating forces
in Scottish life that the figure of Lord James Stewart
adds life and worth to the tale of spiritual freedom
which Scott unveils. Stewart, who afterwards
became Earl of Moray, is acknowledged to be, next
to John Knox, the greatest of the Protestant leaders
of his day. An unbiassed historian such as
Professor Hume Brown has shown that many just
causes created the discontent with Romanism which
Scott so well discloses. We have a memorable
picture of this man in *The Monastery*—his silken
lace, his black velvet bonnet, his pearls and tufted
feather, his sword and gilded spears. More impressive is the outline of his character. It would
be unfair to the novelist to summarise his treatment
of the Regent. The reader will himself place in
his own gallery of great portraits this supplanter
of his sovereign, brave, gifted, ambitious. Principal
Rait has pointed out that he obtained the consent of
Mary for the suppression of the Earl of Huntly.
Queen Elizabeth heard of this gesture to Protestantism. So greatly did this affect Romanism that she
actually spread a rumour in Spain on the strength
of Moray's action, of the lack of devotion on
Moray's part towards Rome. More than a third
of the riches of the country was held by the Church.
Leaders in spiritual authority lived in undue comfort
and ease. Gifts were extracted from those in
poverty. Many of the clergy were unlettered.
They were not fit either to preach or to teach.
When James the Fifth was in need of a teacher,
Sir David Lyndsay was chosen. He used his

poetic gifts justly enough to expose the lack of learning which many of the clergy of that time notoriously revealed. Besides the work of Lindsay and that of the Scriptures, we know that the *Good and Godlie Ballads* had a happy effect later in disseminating the teaching which Mary Avenel learned in her lonely Tower at Glendearg.

The work of Lord James Stewart is made prominent at a later stage in the tale when the Abbot of St. Mary's is seeking means of escape. "He cometh," says the Abbot, "to lay waste and to destroy with his heretic soldiers." The contact which the novelist had with national interests, and with the manner in which feuds between old families affect these wider issues, is seen in the Sub-Prior's reply : "I thought that purpose had been broken by the feud between Semple and the Kennedies." Those who are enamoured of the County of Ayr, and feel the spell of its ballads and history, will the more readily rise to the inwardness of that allusion. Crossraguel Abbey is mentioned in the Abbot's reply, for he knows how well this ancient house was enriched. The Earl of Cassilis he finds is to have the teind-sheaves of the land. These had been given to the house of Crossraguel. The policy of Lord James Stewart had now changed conditions. The matters are settled at the expense of the Church, and to the good of warring lords. The Abbot had a fine sense of the fitness of his Latin Psalter for its use in the exigencies of life—*Principes convenerunt in unum adversus Dominum*. Why did not Sir Walter write a novel on Ayrshire ? Crossraguel, built six hundred years before Scott's death, would have proved a fitting centre. Europe is busy with its crusades, on the rise of the Abbey. If he had not gleaned there matter sufficiently varied from his other novels, he might have taken us to memorable hours in the life of John Knox. In Ochiltree is the place of one romantic episode in the Reformer's life. In historical records the house of the Provost near by the old Collegiate Church in the Capital of Carrick resounds to the thunder of Knox's logic. It may be replied of course that the neighbouring property of Auchendrain was chosen by Scott for a Drama. That work has never held a great place in the estimation of its readers. His reference to Crossraguel when he pictures the doings of Lord James Stewart makes us the more persuaded that under the shadow of its walls, and the neighbouring sentinelship of Ailsa Craig guarding the waters, lies the genesis of such a tale as the Wizard of the North might have aptly told.

The Abbey at Melrose, round which *The Monastery* gathers, was of course more closely under his constant survey than Crossraguel could have been. One of the charms of Melrose to the visitor is to observe the fascinating features of its architecture, on which his eye lovingly lit so often. We think of the window in the chancel with the six crosses, the heart of Douglas with the shaft piercing it, William of Deloraine's door, the groined roof, the images outside the walls, of James the Fourth and Queen Margaret, and a host of features too numerous to detail. We have only to turn to *Lockhart's Life* to learn of the hold that Melrose had upon him. His critics blame him for not making more of his setting. Sometimes it is most difficult to write effectively about the haunts that lay the deepest impress on our hearts, and that we love the most. No words fully express the devotion that he had for its walls. He is blamed too for his seeming unwillingness to take a side in the religious controversy that he makes the theme of this novel. This criticism is without point. For no reader could doubt for a moment where Sir Walter's principles are fixed. The very insistence of his critics on this point is really the unconscious witness to a quality of mind in Sir Walter, almost as enviable as that of " showing our colours." It is the gift too often neglected in these days *of respecting other people's flags*, and the sincerity of their motives in fixing them to the mast. In the truest sense Scott was a member of the Holy Catholic Church.

Interest in these great events, and the desire to mirror in them the experience of the heroes and heroines of the novels, has a fascination. It makes some of the figures that Scott enshrines our life-long companions. We find it worth while, for example, to walk from Melrose to Glendearg. A shepherd who lived in the wildest part of Scotland was so entranced with Sir Walter's description of that place, and the way that leads to it from Melrose, that he wrote to him about it. His letter is dated June 24th, 1820, and he discusses with the novelist in a charming manner the cleughs and ravines of Ettrick, the mystic gambols of the fairies, and the resemblances that he has discovered in his reading of *The Monastery* with features coming before his own observation. He speaks of the overhanging green hills, the dry round knoll with Simon Glendinning's Tower.

The Monastery—and Melrose Abbey

We obtain a happy glimpse of this shepherd. He has tended his sheep for three or four days. No human being is near him. He has entertained himself, so he writes, with *The Monastery*. We feel that in analysis of this novel, sufficient attention is not always paid to the minute carefulness of Scott's work when he describes Nature as it unveils itself around Glendearg. The shepherd's habits brought him into a more reflective mood than is characteristic of our more mechanical age. He was impressed with the excellence of the description of Halbert alighting from the oak with as little injury as the falcon stooping for his meal. He then describes the habits of the eagle, and what he has observed of its flight "in the blue void," its winding course in descent, its approach to its landing stage on some favourite cliff. She alights from her airy flight with as much ease as if she had only been some yards above the ground. The shepherd with his keen perception of the habits of birds was generous enough to tell Sir Walter what this generation perhaps may need to be reminded of. For, in his survey of Nature, as anyone who has walked over the ground of his novels may see, he has faithfully reproduced not alone his wide pageants, but also the minor detail which people who love birds, plants, and little children understand. Is there not a likeness here between Keats, who was a much more rhythmic poet, and Scott? Keats wrote in one of his letters, "I muse on every flower I have known from my infancy—their shape and colour are new to me, as if I had just created them with a superhuman fancy. . . . The simple flowers of our Spring are what I want to see again."

Scott and the Lure of the Road

With this added sense of the worth of Sir Walter's portraiture, we approach Halbert Glendinning's home at Glendearg. If we behold with the shepherd no eagle " like a speck of vapour in the clouds," we at least make our route by the Nameless Dean through which Halbert passed. Sir Walter writes, " Glendearg did not abound in mortal visitants. Superstition that it might not be absolutely destitute of inhabitants peopled its recesses with beings belonging to another world. They were supposed to have formed a residence in a particular wild recess of the glen, of which the real name was in allusion to that circumstance, Corrie-nan-Shian, which in corrupted Celtic signifies the Hollow of the Fairies." Skene has a fine etching of it. The feature of it on which he remarks forms fresh corroboration of Scott's mass of varied knowledge of the surroundings that he describes. Skene shows that the Nameless Dean was noted for the strata of which the banks are composed. Pieces of the substance are worked down by the winter floods, and assume whimsical shapes. He shows that the fresh supply which the storm creates gave to the simple folk who passed there the sense of the supernatural.

> " Spirits, they say,
> Flit round invisible, as thick as motes
> Dance in the sunbeam."

We passed the Dean one Christmastide in the still beauty of a wintry afternoon. It was not difficult under the shadow of the Eildon Hills which Scott loved, and in the solitude of the place, to enter into the experience of Halbert Glendinning when he met the apparition in Corrie-nan-Shian, and received the silver bodkin and the revelation of the inner workings of his mind.

The Glendearg road is very much as the novelist has painted it to us. It bears no witness to the home at the Tower where the events of the book are described. Yet a visit to the locale gives us the sense of atmosphere which is a condition of all appreciation. We can picture the more readily the soldier's family who dwelt there, their difference of taste, and outlook, the hasty nature of Halbert, the gentler mien of Edward, Elspeth their mother made a widow by the horrors of the battle of Pinkie. It was Elspeth's solitariness in Glendearg that possibly prompted her unnatural dread of heresy. She was a vassal of the Kirk. Had she not given Father Philip the precious volume with the silver clasps to get it out of her sight, then perchance its light had sooner proved a guide to Halbert in the faith which he espoused. Scott describes "the Book" as the Church's chiefest treasure. He lays the onus upon the teaching of St. Mary's to which Elspeth adhered, that the Church's gravest loss was her want of an interpreter of that volume, and that its fountain was sealed.

> " Happiest they of human race,
>   To whom God has granted grace,
>   To read, to fear, to hope, to pray."

It would be vain to suggest that in the exponents of the truth of the Reformation, Scott wishes to imply that there was superior courage or morale than was found in the lives of the adherents of St. Mary's. Never in his other works is sternness of principle and unflinching devotion to duty more powerfully conveyed to the reader than in the interview between Henry Warden and the Baron Julian. It was in a castle picturesquely described. It gave the appearance of being completely surrounded by water. He compares it to the nest of a wild swan. He shows how there was one egress, a narrow causeway between the islet and the shore. It is fittingly described by a phrase of James the Sixth when he viewed in Lochwood Castle, the centre of a quaking bog—*Lapis offensionis et petra scandali*. The reader must be left to form his own judgment of that scene. The guilt of a desperate man on the one hand, and the heroism of a godly protester on the other, give the sense of the prophetic which Scott knows so well how to convey. Passages such as this show how Scott's humanism is happily related to his sense of righteousness as it is portrayed in the history of Judaism. We are reminded of the phrase of Professor Butcher, " The influence of Delphi was in no small measure akin to Hebrew prophecy." Warden's attitude shows its kinship with the outlook of the New Testament as well. There is a dignity about Warden, and an unspeakably desperate tone in Julian's attitude that give us one of the enduring pictures of Scott. As Oliver Goldsmith's song has it :

> " When lovely woman stoops to folly,
> And finds too soon that men betray."

We seem again to be in the presence of the Baptist. The hour of recompense has come. The seer in *The Monastery* puts the choice that offers itself to his own conscience in a telling phrase. Is he to hide the light which he is commanded to show forth, or is he to lose the light of this world ? So brave were these men of an ancient faith that he does not hesitate. His choice is made.

We may search in vain round Melrose for the Castle of Avenel. For Scott has added a note to *The Monastery* to tell us that it does not exist as described on his pages. Lochside Tower stands on an islet in Yetholm Loch. It lacks something of the grandeur of the fortress that Scott has painted. In imaginative work such as this, he is able to supersede as all the seers and poets do, thought of time and place. A voice has spoken, and in the echoes of Sir Walter's tones we hear a word divine.

No reader should miss the pedlar episode on the road to Edinburgh. In some ways it is one of the finest passages that Scott wrote in *The Monastery*. Apart from the re-cast it gives of the scene in the Castle, as told by Halbert to the Earl of Moray, it is of interest for its own sake. As we travel by the highway from the Capital to Glasgow, changed as are the conditions to-day, we picture the moss and moor, the hill and dale, and the friendly guidance of the pedlar to the heir of Glendearg, his concealment of his treasures, his pistolet under his cloak in case of need. On the road we seem to hear the echoes of his quaint speech, his defiance of Anti-Christ, his fine sense of caution.

> " And when he came to broken briggs,
> He slack'd his bow and swam,
> And when he came to grass growing,
> Set down his feet and ran."

" Would we to go near these lads of the laird's

belt, your letter would do you little good, and my pack would do me muckle black ill," he exclaims. Halbert could have had no better guardian. The pedlar had the faults of his class, but it was his canny wisdom that enabled Glendinning to brave the horsemen with their glancing casques and twinkling spears. The road which led him to the Earl of Moray's feet is one of the most entrancing paths in a pilgrimage with Scott. For it opens for us the journey of thought to a fascinating period of history, and to the city that Sir Walter loved best on earth.

CHAPTER XIX

THE ABBOT AND KINROSS-SHIRE

In New College days, chaplaincy duty made it possible for the present writer to stay for a summer on the Ochil Hills. The rich table-land spreads itself before us, even in the remembrance of it. Loch Leven lies like a silver shield in the sunlight. It is as if the grim warrior Benarty had cast it at its feet. That mountain lifts its rugged head above it. On the banks of the Loch there nestle little nooks and hamlets associated with the days of which Scott's *Abbot* speaks. In the centre of the wide water stands an island with the ruins of Loch Leven Castle. The fate which shadows the footsteps of the fair Queen of Scots seems to have become part of the continued interest of all patriots. Here she was imprisoned. No one can view the isle without memories crowding on the mind of momentous doings in history. Pity and tears too come readily to the explorer when he pictures the earlier glamour of her Court in France, and in Holyrood with this dark chapter in her story to follow. The loneliness of these fettered hours, the forecast of the coming dawn, the breach with Elizabeth, the treatment meted out to her by her Lords, are recalled. And as sunlight in a winter of gloom there shines the brightness of protecting lives, and loving hearts. Her prison may be bleak and dark, but there are some who are willing to risk something in her honour. There are flowers in the garden of her heart which are the lovelier that in this world of misunderstanding they are rare, and bloom with the sweeter fragrance. Loch Leven Castle is itself a lesson in history. It brings part of a great period before the mind's eye, and in Scott's treatment Mary stands out as an object less for blame than compassion and reverence. Who is not awed in her presence?

> " There beats no heart on either border,
>   Where through the north blasts blow,
> But keeps your memory as a warder,
>   His beacon-fires aglow."

Through these pages we have sought to win the reader to ally each country to its literary lore. No countryside lends itself so fittingly to the novelist's hand as the district of Kinross. Sojourn in it has the advantage that sight of a miniature has. Æsthetically it is sometimes of advantage to find peace and beauty in small compass. Those who have passed unforgettable hours in that romantic district will be the first to admit the magnetism of these surroundings on the soul of the artist who depicts the struggles and the imprison-ment of our poor deluded Queen. Here again we have proof that Scott knew well the ground over which he asks the reader to travel. Lockhart says that the novelist had owned to him that the idea of the *Abbot* had arisen in the author's mind on a visit to Blair-Adam. It was here that a great friend, Commissioner Adam, lived, who held a

The Abbot and Loch Leven

judgeship in the Court of Session. He was frequently the host of Scott at his beautiful home, from which Loch Leven Castle could be seen. Adam writes of these visits, and of these literary comrades lying on the grassy summit of Benarty. He admits that the Castle was the most renowned in the neighbourhood, and that Scott by his creative fancy cast a deeper sense of feeling into the story of Mary's captivity and escape. Possibly, the realism of the tale may partly account for its success. Mr. Morritt wrote from Rokeby in 1820 to tell Scott that the *Abbot* is extremely popular. He says, " Two or three of my correspondents are in raptures over it. I thought Queen Mary would take, and rejoice in my sagacity." This testimony is the more noteworthy when we recall the confidence that Scott had in Morritt. He was one of the very few to whom he gave the secret of the authorship of the Waverley Novels.

Buchan regards Mary as the best of Scott's illustrious women in history. There are many who share this critic's view. She is not easy to portray. For her character was as varied as this changing world in which we live. She had a magnetism that drew contemporaries to her, as well as a charm that makes the succeeding ages feel her sway. Adam Woodcock describes the match between Bothwell and the Baron of Roslin. It would be difficult to excel him in his phrasing as he describes the Queen : " To see her there on her white palfrey that flew as if it scorned to touch more than the heather blossom ; and to hear her voice, as clear and sweet as the mavis's whistle, mix among our jolly whoop and whistling ; and to mark all the nobles dashing round her, happiest he who got a word or a look, tearing through moss and hagg, and venturing neck and limb to gain the praise of a bold rider, and the blink of the bonny Queen's bright eye."

What entices us to the background that the Author so richly paints? How does it fit into the picture of the period? The most obvious answer to these queries is that the ground here is historically correct. When Scott represents the stirring eras of this novel, his general conception is in accord with the doings of that era. Scotland was in some peril of changing its faith. The Reformation had accomplished its noble work, and yet it could not claim to have been fully confirmed. The very thunder of John Knox's voice in St. Giles' Cathedral was a testimony to the menace that he knew faced the country. Holyroodhouse, which to-day is so advantageously allied with the spirit and creed of the Church of Scotland, was at the period of Queen Mary a centre of somewhat divisive forces. The Court life, the practice of Mass, the adventurous figures, such as Bothwell, Darnley and Rizzio, whose company dazzled life in high places, made Reformers somewhat suspicious. Would Mary be successful in introducing Romanism within the realm? Would she reign with too little regard for the feelings and traditions of the Scottish people? Lord Lindsay, Lord Ruthven and the rest were uneasy as they thought of her future rule. If she were to continue in power, then her authority must be balanced by the wishes of the dominant party in the State. Scott does not give in detail the genesis of the tragedy that led to her imprisonment. But the study of this fascinating novel leads earnest students to examine the period with thoroughness. None but the most biassed student, whatever his views of the political and religious situation, can be devoid of a deep sense of pity for her as she suffers there. It is a disastrous change, that lonely fortress, from the gaiety of Holyrood, and her earlier irresponsible youth in France. If she were never quite at home among the Scots, how could she learn to bear with them when their hand was raised against her ? She had never been in subjection. It was the more difficult for her when not only her body, but her mind was in bondage. It is to be questioned whether the most understanding of her advisers really knew how to treat a sensitive woman, what nobler motives to stir in her heart, what fears to allay, what high impulses to prompt. They treated her sometimes with less than the gentleness that makes men great. It is true that she seemed to belittle the worth of principles dear to them. Yet she had held a different faith, and lived in an alien atmosphere. She was the object also of the wrath of Elizabeth, and here on this lonely isle in a desolate part of Scotland what influences were at work to lead her to change her outlook ? If Loch Leven were chosen to accomplish any reformation in her, was it the most likely school of repentance ?

But even there she had friends. The Regent Murray might well imagine her in security that was undoubted. But Roland was willing to plan for her, and there were sympathetic hearts such as that of Lady Fleming that came to his aid. He had been interested in the work of the anvil. It

was an easy matter for him to fashion articles of
passing worth to give as gifts to the household,
or to spend recreative hours in the armoury, and
at his tools.   In this way, suspicion was prevented.
Hour by hour, in concealment, he made a duplicate
of the keys.   The nightly task of an attendant was
to lay the real keys on the table beside the lady in
waiting.   Quickly he changed them for those that
he had fashioned.   Warning was given, the boat
launched, and the Queen safely landed on the other
side of the water.   Loch Leven lends itself to
dramatic representation such as Scott gives to the
scene.   We can picture the clang of these barred
doors, as Roland locks them on the outside, the
alarm of the residents as they hear the swish of the
oars on the water.   Andrew Lang's *Essay* on the
novel may give rise to criticism for a somewhat
unfriendly attitude to certain aspects of Protestantism, but every reader will be at one with him
in his comments on the effectiveness of Scott in the
scene that we have described.   " Necessarily," he
writes, " he admired and pitied that unfortunate
lady, cradled in defeat, destined to a task perfectly
hopeless and impossible, beset by every temptation,
betrayed on every hand.   Her beauty, her grace, her
courage, her steadfast loyalty to her creed, raise the
Queen high above the tumult of turbulent lords,
who alternately supported and deserted her."
The " Quarterly," at the time when *The Abbot* was
published, made this salient summary—" Queen
Mary has at length fallen into the hands of an
Author that deserves her."

Readers who linger over the scene of the escape
must have been fascinated by the description of the

The Abbot and Loch Leven

light in the dwelling in Kinross. Some heart there was loyal to the imprisoned lady. Someone there was willing to risk much to bring her to safety. In dark days in the Castle on the isle the inspiration of that light was like an impulse, divine in the soul of Roland. Still on these fair country roads they point us to the little bridge over which she was reputed to cross. If we make our westward way we can see the scene of the battlefield of Langside, now a suburb of Glasgow, to which the ill-fated Queen rode these strenuous days. There are those who place the escape from the Castle as the second best scene in the plot. Possibly the light and shade which the fair surroundings in Kinross-shire lend it add much to the picturesqueness of the setting. If the signing of the royal deed of demission is the premier scene, it is portrayed in so grim an environment of closed walls that it hardly comes within our scope. But it is linked in unbroken memory in our thought of *The Abbot*. It is moulded too in Scott's thought with as great an era in the life of Richard the Second.

> " I give this heavy weight from off my head,
> And this unwieldy sceptre from my hand ;
> With mine own tears, I wash away my balm,
> With mine own hand, I give away my crown,
> With mine own tongue deny my sacred state,
> With mine own breath release all duteous oaths."

There is a tradition that Queen Mary found shelter in the Abbey of Dundrennan in that secluded corner of Galloway, sixty miles from the battlefield of Langside. It is an attractive theory. For, with map in hand, we can readily trace the journey which Lord Herries described through Sanquhar, and if we look across the Solway from Port Mary, we can easily imagine her amid the peace of that Abbey, sheltered by its ministers of peace. We see her, as Scott pictures her, amongst the flowers beside old Ambrose, who had been one of her chivalrous friends in Kinross in days when still there lingered the hope in brave hearts that she might evade her persecutors. Scott at all events did not disbelieve the tradition of her brief sojourn at Dundrennan, although it is doubted by those who have tested the sources. It is a tender parting with which he ends his tale. They watch the vessel till in size it becomes as small as a child's toy sailing-boat. Not till then do the sorrowful followers part on the sands. Their last sight at Port Mary is the Queen's little white kerchief, and we wave her adieu. We cannot say farewell to Sir Walter, and if the reader should desire further light on his journeys along paths which the figures in other novels have travelled, we shall attempt to win him anew to Scott and to the Lure of the Road.

BIBLIOGRAPHY

Bagehot. *Essay on Scott.*
Boswell. *Tour to the Hebrides.*
Brown-Hume. *History of Scotland.*
Buchan, John. *Life of Scott.*
Cameron, S. Wallis. *The Valley of the Silent Loch.*
Canning, the Hon. S. G. *Scott and his Novels.*
Christie. *Week-End Scott.*
Crockett. *Scott Originals.*
Crockett, W. S. *Scott Country.*
Dawson, W. J. *Makers of English Fiction.*
Dick, W. M. A. *Byron and his Poetry.*
Dickson, Nicholas. *The Bible in Waverley.*
Douglas Book.
Dryden, Sir Henry, Bart. *Saint Magnus.*
Gosse, Dr. Edmund. *Modern English Literature.*
Graham, Henry. *Scottish Men of Letters in the Eighteenth Century.*
Grierson. *Cross Currents in English Literature.*
Gunn, Winifred. *The Moving Hand.* A Dramatic Representation.
Harnack. *Monasticism.*
Hazlitt. *Essay on Scott.*
Heddle and Muirhead, F.E.W. *County Geography of Orkney and Shetland*
Hegel. *Philosophy of History.*
Henderson. *Religion in Scotland. Its Influence on National Character.*
Herford, Professor. *Age of Wordsworth.*
Hogg. *Poems.*
Hogg, James. *Famous Scots Series.*
Husband, M. F. A., M.A. *Dictionary of Waverley Novels.*
Hutchison, Douglas J. D., B.Sc. *Church of St. Bride.*
Irving, Washington. *Essay on Scott.*
James, Sir Henry. *Essay on Scott.*
Jeffrey. *Edinburgh Review.*

Bibliography

Johnson, Samuel. *Tour to the Hebrides.*

Lang, Andrew. *The Poet's Country.*

Lang, Andrew. *The Poetical Works.*

Lang, Andrew. *Border Edition of Scott and Introductory Essays.*

Lang, Andrew and John. *Highways and Byways of the Border.*

Lockhart. *Life of Scott.*

MacEwen, Professor. *Scottish Church History.*

McCormick. *Tinker Gypsies.*

Mudie. *Scott and the Lure of the Road.*

Muirhead, Findlay, M.A., F.R.C.S. *The Blue Guide to England and Scotland.*

Paterson. *Life of Joseph Train.*

Patten. *Character Study.*

Pet Marjorie's Diary. *Edited by Dr. Archibald Fleming.*

Philip, Dr. Adam. *Devotional Literature of Scotland.*

Rait, Principal. *Mary Queen of Scots. Extracts from State Papers.*

Rait. *History of Scotland.*

Robertson, Logie. *Poetry and Verse from the Waverley Novels.*

Saintsbury. *Famous Scots Series.*

Scott. *Journal.*

Scott. *Lives of British Novelists.*

Scott. *Minstrelsy of the Scottish Borders.*

Skene. *A Series of Sketches of Existing Localities.*

Walpole, Hugh. *The Private Letters of Scott.*

Watson. *The Statute Laws of the XV and XVI Centuries.*

Willcock, Dr. Archibald. *Earl of Argyll.*

Printed at the BURLEIGH PRESS, *Lewin's Mead,* BRISTOL